Guitar Adventures

A Fun, Informative, and Step–By–Step 60–Lesson Guide

Damon Ferrante

Guitar Adventures: A Fun, Informative,
and Step-By-Step 60-Lesson Guide to Chords,
Beginner & Intermediate Levels,
with Companion Lesson-
and Play-Along Videos

by Damon Ferrante

For additional information about
music books, recordings, and concerts,
please visit the Steeplechase website:
www.steeplechasearts.com

steeplechase

arts & productions

ISBN-13:
978-1479106196

ISBN-10:
1479106194

Introduction

How the Book Works

> ❖**Check Out**
> **Video Lesson 1:**
> **Introduction**

The Book

This book follows a step-by-step lesson format for learning how to play chords on the guitar. Each lesson builds on the previous one in a clear and easy-to-understand manner. There are 61 lessons in the book. A lesson checklist at the end of the book helps you keep track of your progress and plan out your practice goals. You learn the chords through songs, which you can play along with on the <u>free</u>, Play-Along Videos.

At the end of the book, you will be able to play the following chords in every key: Major, Minor, Dominant Seventh, Minor Seventh, Augmented, Diminished, Barre Chords, and Power Chords. These are the most useful and common chords for all styles and genres of music.

The Videos

There are 2 types of videos in this book: The Video Lessons and the Play-Along Videos. There are 10 Video Lessons, which demonstrate the playing techniques and concepts featured in the book, for example, how major and minor chords are formed, how to play power chords and barre chords, and how to locate notes on the guitar neck. There are 8 Play-Along Videos, which enable you to play along with songs featured in the book. All of these videos are <u>free</u> and available on <u>Youtube</u> at the <u>GuitarAdventures</u> <u>Channel</u>. <u>No</u> Registration or Sign-Up is needed to view the videos and there is no limit to the amount of times that they may be viewed.

Table of Contents

Symbols used in this book

Left-Hand Symbols:

(1) · 1st Finger (Index Finger)

(2) · 2nd Finger (Middle Finger)

(3) · 3rd Finger (Ring Finger)

(4) · 4th Finger (Pinky Finger)

(—) · Place Finger over 2 or more strings.

O · Open String (Let the String Vibrate.)

X · Mute String (Block the String with a Finger.)

Instructional Videos:

· There are 18 Supplemental Instructional Videos that correspond to the lessons in this Book.
· The Videos provide additional instruction and play-along recordings.
· These Videos are Free and Available on Youtube at the GuitarAdventures Channel
· No Registration is needed to view the Videos and there is no limit to the amount of times they may be viewed.

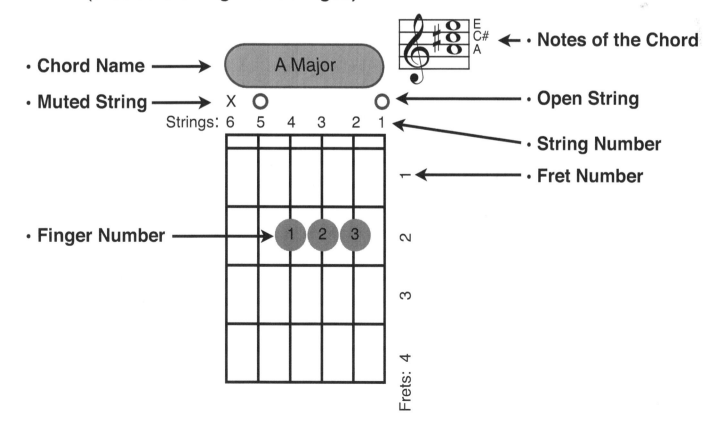

· Chord Name ⟶ A Major

· Notes of the Chord

· Muted String ⟶ X O   O ⟵ · Open String

Strings: 6 5 4 3 2 1 ⟵ · String Number

⟵ · Fret Number

· Finger Number ⟶ (1)(2)(3)

Frets: 4

Section 1

Major Chords:
Open Position

Lesson 1
Major Chords: Open Position

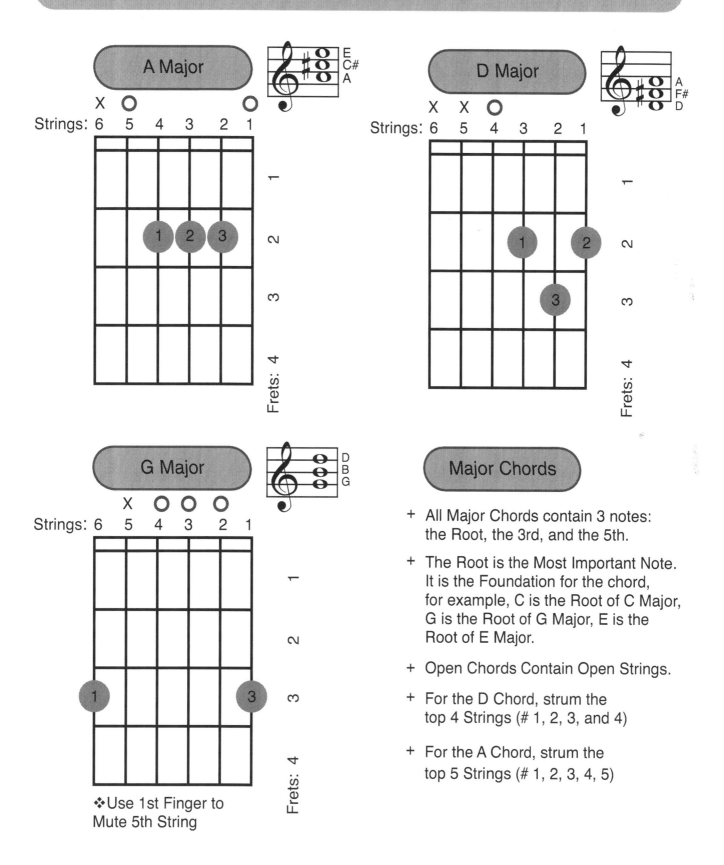

A Major

E
C#
A

Strings: 6 5 4 3 2 1
X O   O

Frets: 1 2 3 4

D Major

A
F#
D

Strings: 6 5 4 3 2 1
X X O

Frets: 1 2 3 4

G Major

D
B
G

Strings: 6 5 4 3 2 1
   X O O O

Frets: 1 2 3 4

❖Use 1st Finger to
Mute 5th String

Major Chords

+ All Major Chords contain 3 notes: the Root, the 3rd, and the 5th.

+ The Root is the Most Important Note. It is the Foundation for the chord, for example, C is the Root of C Major, G is the Root of G Major, E is the Root of E Major.

+ Open Chords Contain Open Strings.

+ For the D Chord, strum the top 4 Strings (# 1, 2, 3, and 4)

+ For the A Chord, strum the top 5 Strings (# 1, 2, 3, 4, 5)

Lesson 2
Amazing Grace

Amazing Grace

Measure Line

Chord:	D	D	G	D
	A-mazing	Grace how	sweet the	sound that
Strum:	1 2 3	1 2 3	1 2 3	1 2 3

Chord:	D	D	A	A
	saved a	wretch like	me.	I
Strum:	1 2 3	1 2 3	1 2 3	1 2 3

Chord:	D	D	G	D
	once was	lost but	now am	found. Was
Strum:	1 2 3	1 2 3	1 2 3	1 2 3

Chord:	D	A	D	D
	blind but	now I	see.	
Strum:	1 2 3	1 2 3	1 2 3	1 2 3

Measures

+ Music is composed of groups of beats called measures.

+ Measures are set off by two vertical lines.

+ Measures most commonly contain 2, 3, or 4 beats.

+ Our first song, *Amazing Grace,* has 3 beats in each measure.

+ Strum the chords of *Amazing Grace* 3 times for each measure.

+ Start strumming on the second syllable of the word "Amazing".

Amazing *Grace*

+ *Amazing Grace uses* the D, G, and A major chords.

+ The chords are shown above the words.

+ The beats (or strum patterns) are shown below the words.

+ Practice each line slowly, while singing the words aloud or in your head.

+ Try forming a chord once and strum. Then, place your left hand on your lap and repeat the process for each chord 10-20 times.

Lesson 3
Major Chords: Open Position

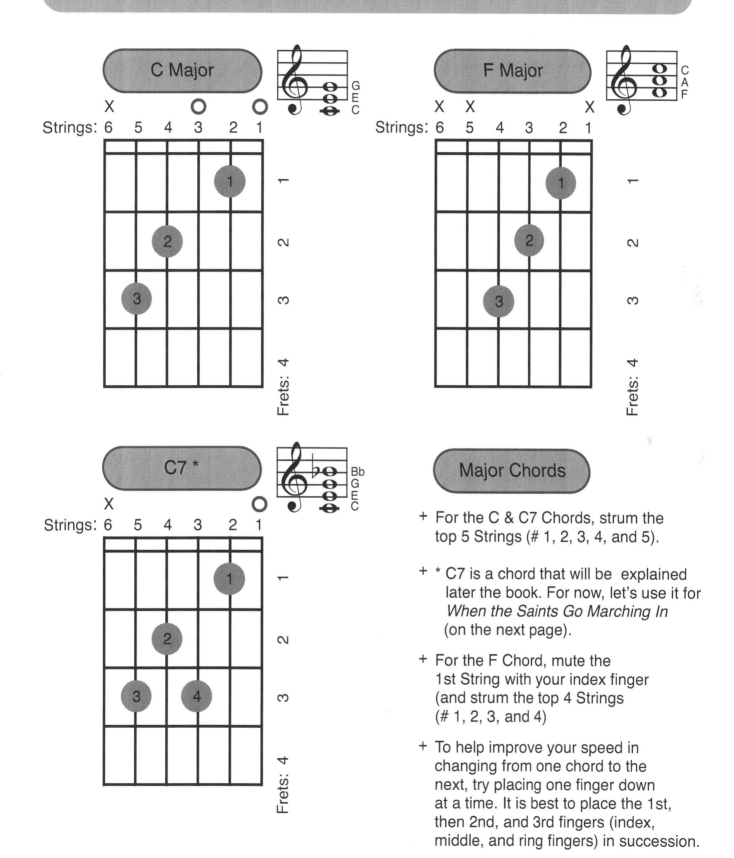

Major Chords

+ For the C & C7 Chords, strum the top 5 Strings (# 1, 2, 3, 4, and 5).

+ * C7 is a chord that will be explained later the book. For now, let's use it for *When the Saints Go Marching In* (on the next page).

+ For the F Chord, mute the 1st String with your index finger (and strum the top 4 Strings (# 1, 2, 3, and 4)

+ To help improve your speed in changing from one chord to the next, try placing one finger down at a time. It is best to place the 1st, then 2nd, and 3rd fingers (index, middle, and ring fingers) in succession.

Lesson 4
When the Saints Go Marching In

When the Saints

Chord:	(No Chord)		C		C		C
	Oh When the		Saints		go marchin'		in
Strum: 1 2 3 4			1 2 3 4		1 2 3 4		1 2 3 4
Chord: C			C		C7		G
	Oh When the		Saints go		marchin'		in
Strum: 1 2 3 4			1 2 3 4		1 2 3 4		1 2 3 4
Chord: G			C		C7		F
	Oh Lord, I		want to		be in that		number
Strum: 1 2 3 4			1 2 3 4		1 2 3 4		1 2 3 4
Chord: F			C		G		C
	Oh When the		Saints go		marchin'		in
Strum: 1 2 3 4			1 2 3 4		1 2 3 4		1 2 3 4

Upbeats

+ In music, there are many songs and pieces that use upbeats.

+ An upbeat (or upbeats) are notes that occur before the first full measure of a song.

+ Upbeats act as a very short introductory phrases that emphasize an important note or word at the beginning of a song. For example, in *When the Saints Go Marchin' In,* the words "Oh when the" are the upbeat. They lead into and accentuate the word "saints".

When the *Saints*

+ *When the Saints uses* the C, F, and G major chords.

+ The chords are shown above the words.

+ The beats (or strum patterns) are show below the words.

+ Practice each line slowly, while singing the words aloud or in your head.

+ If you cannot remember one of the chords, review the chord diagrams on the previous pages.

+ Strum the Chords 4 times for each measure.

Lesson 5
Major Chords: Open Position

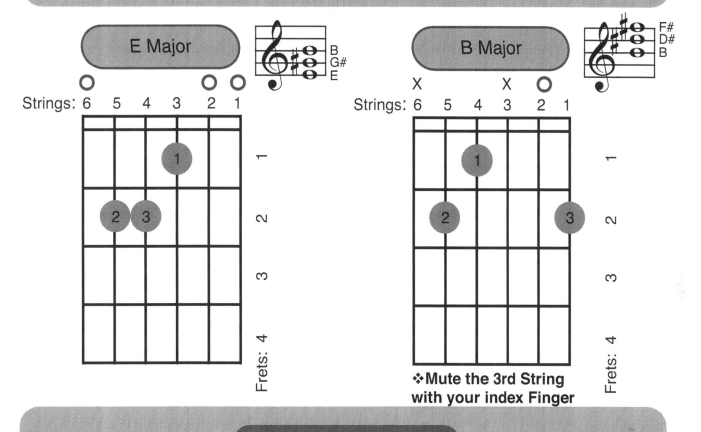

E Major

Strings: 6 5 4 3 2 1

Frets: 4

B Major

Strings: 6 5 4 3 2 1

Frets: 4

❖Mute the 3rd String
with your index Finger

Peace Like a River

Chord: (No Chord)	E	E	A
I've got	peace like a	river. I've got	Peace like a
Strum: 1 2 3 4	1 2 3 4	1 2 3 4	1 2 3 4
Chord: E	E	E	B
river. I've got	peace like a	river in my	soul.
Strum: 1 2 3 4	1 2 3 4	1 2 3 4	1 2 3 4
Chord: B	E	E	A
I've got	Peace like a	river. I've got	peace like a
Strum: 1 2 3 4	1 2 3 4	1 2 3 4	1 2 3 4
Chord: E	E	B	E
river. I've got	peace like a	river in my	soul.
Strum: 1 2 3 4	1 2 3 4	1 2 3 4	1 2 3 4

Lesson 6
Let's Look Back:

D, G, & A Chords

+ Play though *When the Saints Go Marching In* using the D, G, & A major chords, instead of the C, F, and G major chords.

+ Go back to Lesson 4: *When the Saints Go Marching In*

+ When you see a C, play a D instead.

+ When you see a C7, play a D instead.

+ When you see a G, play an A instead.

+ When you see an F, play a G instead.

+ At first, try this very slowly.

Major Chords

+ Find other songs that use these Major Chords.

+ Try playing through the songs in this section using different strumming patterns. For example, try these:

+ Down Up Down Up

+ Down Down Up Down

Have Fun!

C, F, & G Chords

+ *Play Amazing Grace* using the C, F, and G major chords, instead of D, G, and A major chords.

+ Go back to Lesson 2: *Amazing Grace*

+ When you see a D, play a C instead.

+ When you see a G, play an F instead.

+ When you see an A, play G instead.

+ At first, try this very slowly. Then, gradually increase the speed.

Moving Forward

On the Following Page:

Ⓡ Stands for Root

③ Stands for 3rd

⑤ Stands for 5th

O Means let the string vibrate

X Means mute the string with a Left-Hand Finger.

Before Moving Forward, make sure that you are comfortable with the material from Chapter 1, if not take a few days to review the material before going to Chapter 2.

Lesson 7: Overview
Major & Minor Chords

Intervals

+ Chords are formed by playing several different notes on the guitar at the same time.

+ The distances between these notes are called "intervals".

+ The most basic interval (or distance between notes) is called a "second".

+ There are 2 types of second intervals: minor and major.

+ On the guitar, the easiest way to understand these intervals is to look at the fretboard.

+ If you put one finger on the 1st fret and another on the 2nd fret, that is the distance of a minor second. If you put one finger on the 1st fret and another on the 3rd fret, that is the distance of a major second.

Major & Minor Chords

+ All Major & Minor Chords contain 3 notes: the Root, the 3rd, and the 5th.

+ In Major Chords the distance between the Root and the 3rd is made up of 2 Major 2nds.

+ In Minor Chords the distance between the Root and the 3rd is made up of 1 Major 2nd and 1 Minor 2nd.

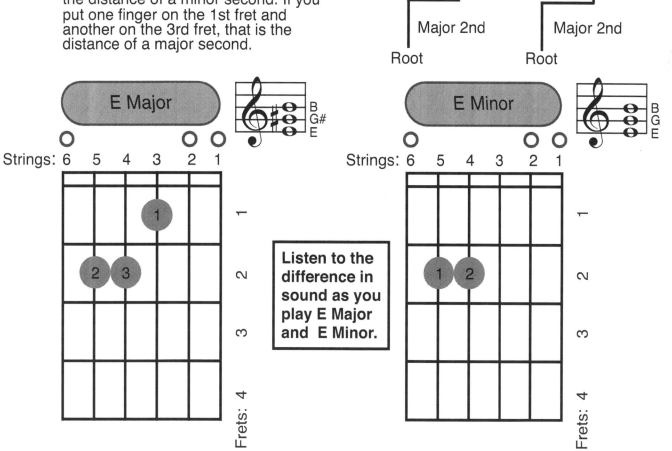

Listen to the difference in sound as you play E Major and E Minor.

What We Have Learned: Section 1

- Open-Position Major Chords: A, B, C, D, E, F, G

- *Amazing Grace*

- *When the Saints Go Marching In*

- *Peace Like a River*

- The Structure of Major Chords

- The Structure of Minor Chords

- Basic Beats, Rhythms, and Strumming Patterns

Check Out These Artists Who Use Major Chords

- U2: *Where the Streets Have No Name*

- Bob Dylan: *Tangled Up in Blue*

- Bruno Mars: *Grenade*

- Lady Gaga: *Edge of Glory*

- The Cure: *Just Like Heaven*

Section 2

Minor Chords:
Open Position

Lesson 8
Minor Chords: Open Position

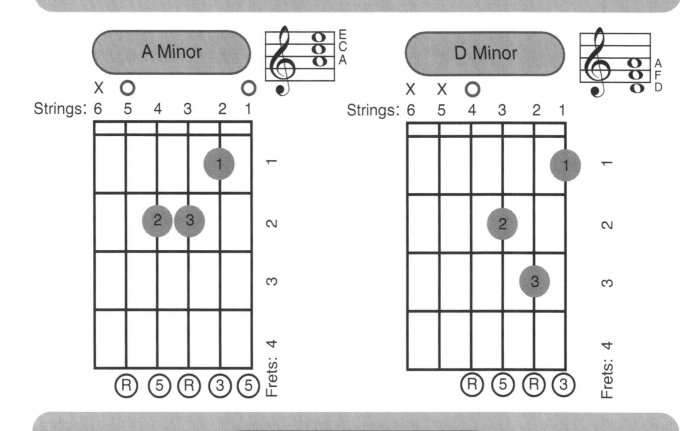

House of the Rising Sun

Chord:	**Am**	**C**	**D**	**F**
	There is a	house in	New Or-	leans they
Strum:	1 2 3	1 2 3	1 2 3	1 2 3

Chord:	**Am**	**C**	**E**	**E**
	call the	ris- ing	sun.	It's
Strum:	1 2 3	1 2 3	1 2 3	1 2 3

Chord:	**Am**	**C**	**D**	**F**
	been the	ruin of	many poor	souls and
Strum:	1 2 3	1 2 3	1 2 3	1 2 3

Chord:	**Am**	**E**	**Am**	**Am**
	Lord, I	know I'm	one.	
Strum:	1 2 3	1 2 3	1 2 3	1 2 3

Lesson 9
Minor Chords: Open Position

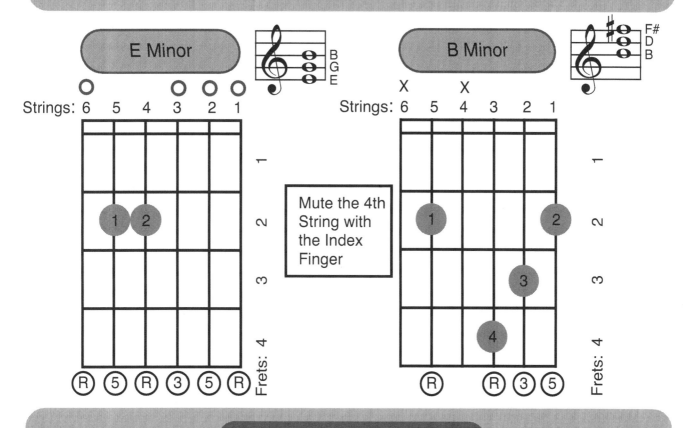

E Minor — B G E

Strings: 6 5 4 3 2 1

Ⓞ ⃝ Ⓞ Ⓞ Ⓞ

1 2

Ⓡ ⑤ Ⓡ ③ ⑤ Ⓡ Frets: 1 2 3 4

Mute the 4th String with the Index Finger

B Minor — F# D B

X X

Strings: 6 5 4 3 2 1

1 2

3

4

Ⓡ Ⓡ ③ ⑤ Frets: 1 2 3 4

Scarborough Fair

Chord:	Em	G	D	Em	Em
	Are you	going to	Scarborough	Fair?	
Strum:	1 2 3	1 2 3	1 2 3	1 2 3	1 2 3
Chord:	G	Em	A	Em	Em
	Parsley	Sage Rose-	mary and	thyme	Oh,
Strum:	1 2 3	1 2 3	1 2 3	1 2 3	1 2 3
Chord:	Em	G	C	D	D
	send my	love to	one who lives	there.	For
Strum:	1 2 3	1 2 3	1 2 3	1 2 3	1 2 3
Chord:	Em	D	C	Em	Em
	she once	was a	true love of	mine.	
Strum:	1 2 3	1 2 3	1 2 3	1 2 3	1 2 3

Lesson 10
Minor Chords: Open Position

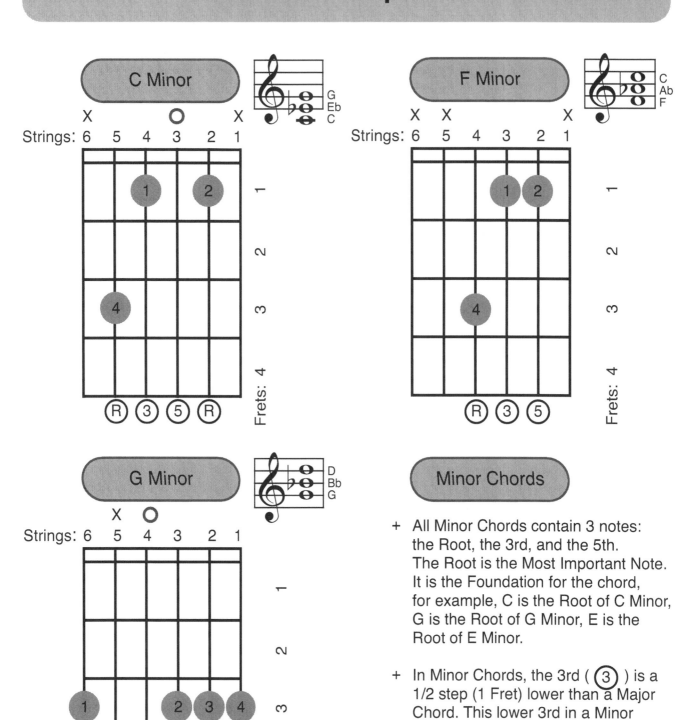

C Minor

G
Eb
C

X   O   X

Strings: 6   5   4   3   2   1

1   2

4

Frets: 1   2   3   4

Ⓡ ③ ⑤ Ⓡ

F Minor

C
Ab
F

X   X   X

Strings: 6   5   4   3   2   1

1   2

4

Frets: 1   2   3   4

Ⓡ ③ ⑤

G Minor

D
Bb
G

X   O

Strings: 6   5   4   3   2   1

1   2   3   4

Frets: 1   2   3   4

Ⓡ ⑤ ③ ⑤ Ⓡ

Use 1st Finger to
Mute 5th String

Minor Chords

+ All Minor Chords contain 3 notes:
  the Root, the 3rd, and the 5th.
  The Root is the Most Important Note.
  It is the Foundation for the chord,
  for example, C is the Root of C Minor,
  G is the Root of G Minor, E is the
  Root of E Minor.

+ In Minor Chords, the 3rd (③) is a
  1/2 step (1 Fret) lower than a Major
  Chord. This lower 3rd in a Minor
  Chord gives it the "Minor" sound
  quality.

+ In general, Minor Chords have a
  bittersweet or more somber character
  than Major Chords (which tend to
  sound brighter).

Lesson 11
Let's Look Back, Minor Chords:

E Minor

+ Play though *House of the Rising Sun* using the E Minor, A Minor, B, C, and G Major Chords.

+ Go back to Lesson 8: *House of the Rising Sun*

+ When you see Am, play a Em instead.

+ When you see a C, play an G instead.

+ When you see an F, play a C instead.

+ When you see an E, play a B instead.

+ At first, try this very slowly.

Strumming

+ As you Play through *House of the Rising Sun* using these different chords, try gently strumming the chords with the nails of your right-hand fingers.

+ Listen to the difference in sound between the fingernails and the pick.

+ Keep a loose wrist while strumming. This will give your chords a better sound and improve your rhythm.

+ If you have trouble making a transition to certain chords, isolate the 2 tricky chords. Then, alternate playing them very slowly.

Minor Chords

+ Find other songs that use these Minor Chords.

+ Try playing through *House of the Rising Sun* using different strumming patterns. For example, try these:

+ Down Up Down

+ Down Down Up

Have Fun!

Greensleeves

+ On the Following Page:

+ Greensleeves:

+ There are 3 strums (or beats) in each measure of Greensleeves.

+ The first beat of each measure is called the "downbeat".

+ Try to give more emphasis to the first strum ("downbeat") in each measure.

+ By slightly accenting the downbeat of each measure, you will provide a stronger rhythm to the song.

Lesson 12
Greensleeves

Verse Section   *Greensleeves*

Chord:	**Am**	**Am**	**G**	**G**	**Am**
	A-las my	love, you	do me	wrong to	cast me
Strum:	1 2 3	1 2 3	1 2 3	1 2 3	1 2 3

Chord:	**Am**	**E**	**E**	**Am**	**Am**
	off dis-	courteous-	ly when	I have	loved
Strum:	1 2 3	1 2 3	1 2 3	1 2 3	1 2 3

Chord:	**G**	**G**	**Am**	**E**	**Am**
	you so	long, de-	light- ing	in your	com-pan-
Strum:	1 2 3	1 2 3	1 2 3	1 2 3	1 2 3

Chord:	**Am**	
	y	**Chorus Section (Go to the Next Line)**
Strum:	1 2 3	

Chord:	**C**	**C**	**G**	**G**
	Green	Sleeves was	all my	joy and
Strum:	1 2 3	1 2 3	1 2 3	1 2 3

Chord:	**Am**	**Am**	**E**	**E**
	Green	Sleeves was	my de-	light.
Strum:	1 2 3	1 2 3	1 2 3	1 2 3

Chord:	**C**	**C**	**G**	**G**
	Green	Sleeves was	heart of	gold and
Strum:	1 2 3	1 2 3	1 2 3	1 2 3

Chord:	**Am**	**E**	**Am**	**Am**
	who but my	lady	Green	Sleeves.
Strum:	1 2 3	1 2 3	1 2 3	1 2 3

What We Have Learned: Section 2

- Open-Position Minor Chords: A, B, C, D, E, F, G

- *House of the Rising Sun*

- *Scarborough Fair*

- *Greensleeves*

- The Structure of Minor Chords, continued

- Combining Major and Minor Chords in the Same Song

Check Out These Artists Who Use Minor Chords

- The Beatles: *Eleanor Rigby*

- Bruce Springsteen: *The River*

- Foo Fighters: *Walk*

- Aerosmith: *Dream On*

Section 3

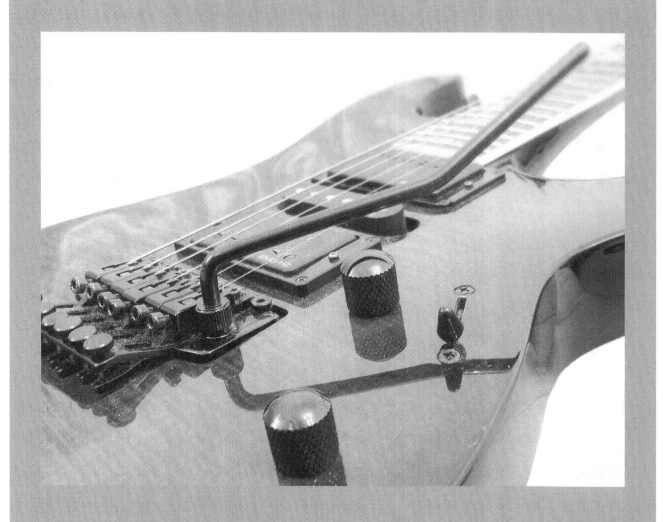

Dominant 7th Chords:
Open Position

Lesson 13: Dominant 7th Chords
Open Position

❖Check Out
Video Lesson 4

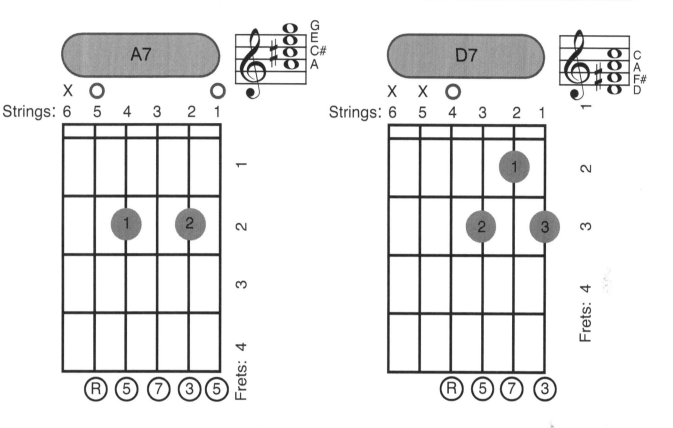

A7

G
E
C#
A

X	O				O
Strings: 6	5	4	3	2	1

Fret 2: 1 (string 4), 2 (string 2)

Frets: 1 2 3 4

(R) (5) (7) (3) (5)

D7

C
A
F#
D

X	X	O			
Strings: 6	5	4	3	2	1

Fret 1: 1 (string 2)
Fret 2: 2 (string 3), 3 (string 1)

Frets: 2 3 4

(R) (5) (7) (3)

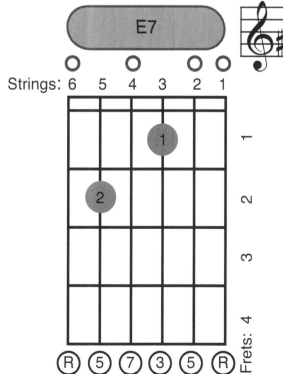

E7

D
B
G#
E

O	O		O		O
Strings: 6	5	4	3	2	1

Fret 1: 1 (string 3)
Fret 2: 2 (string 5)

Frets: 1 2 3 4

(R) (5) (7) (3) (5) (R)

Dominant 7th Chords

+ All Dominant 7th Chords contain 4 notes: the Root, the 3rd, 5th and the 7th: (R) (3) (5) (7)

+ The Root is the Most Important Note. It is the Foundation for the chord, for example, C is the Root of C7 and G is the Root of G7.

+ Dominant 7th Chords are often abbreviated with the Chord Letter and the Number 7. For example, A7 and D7 stand for A Dominant Seventh Chord and D Dominant Seventh Chord.

+ Dominant 7th Chords have a "bluesy" quality and can "spice" up Major Chords.

Lesson 14
12-Bar Blues Progression

In A   12-Bar Blues

Chord:	A7	A7	A7	A7
Strum:	1 2 3 4	1 2 3 4	1 2 3 4	1 2 3 4

Chord:	D7	D7	A7	A7
Strum:	1 2 3 4	1 2 3 4	1 2 3 4	1 2 3 4

Chord:	E7	D7	A7	A7
Strum:	1 2 3 4	1 2 3 4	1 2 3 4	1 2 3 4

12-Bar Blues

+ In music the word "bar" means "measure".

+ Many Blues, Rock, and Jazz songs use a 12-measure (or "12-Bar") format. For this format, you play the 12 measures and then return to the beginning and repeat them again.

+ After you have played through the "12-Bar Blues" a few times with 4 strums per measure, try experimenting with different strumming patterns and rhythms.

Have fun!

On the Next Page

+ Rockabilly is a mix of Blues, Rock, Jazz and Country. It was popularized in the 1950s by artists like Elvis and Chuck Berry.

+ Two good examples of the style are *Hound Dog* by Elvis and *Johnny Be Good* by Chuck Berry.

+ Our Rockabilly Lessons (on the next few pages) involve chord patterns played on only 2 adjacent strings.

+ When playing these Lessons, try to isolate each 2-string chord and make short strums with your Right Hand.

Lesson 15:
Rockabilly Progression, Part 1

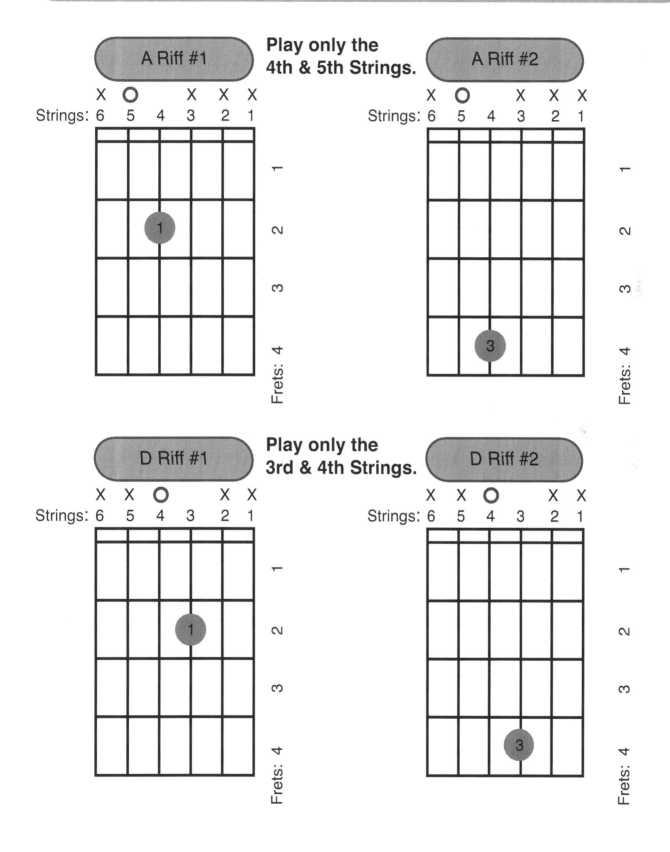

A Riff #1

Play only the 4th & 5th Strings.

A Riff #2

D Riff #1

Play only the 3rd & 4th Strings.

D Riff #2

Lesson 16:
Rockabilly Progression, Part 2

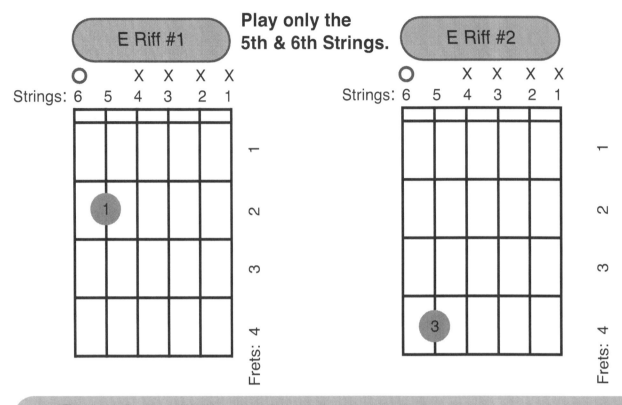

E Riff #1

**Play only the
5th & 6th Strings.**

E Riff #2

For each measure, alternate between Riff 1 & 2.

12-Bar Blues

Chord:	A Riff 1 & 2	A Riff 1 & 2	A Riff 1 & 2	A Riff 1 & 2
Strum:	1 2 3 4	1 2 3 4	1 2 3 4	1 2 3 4
Chord:	D Riff 1 & 2	D Riff 1 & 2	A Riff 1 & 2	A Riff 1 & 2
Strum:	1 2 3 4	1 2 3 4	1 2 3 4	1 2 3 4
Chord:	E Riff 1 & 2	D Riff 1 & 2	A Riff 1 & 2	A Riff 1 & 2
Strum:	1 2 3 4	1 2 3 4	1 2 3 4	1 2 3 4

Lesson 17: Dominant 7th Chords Open Position

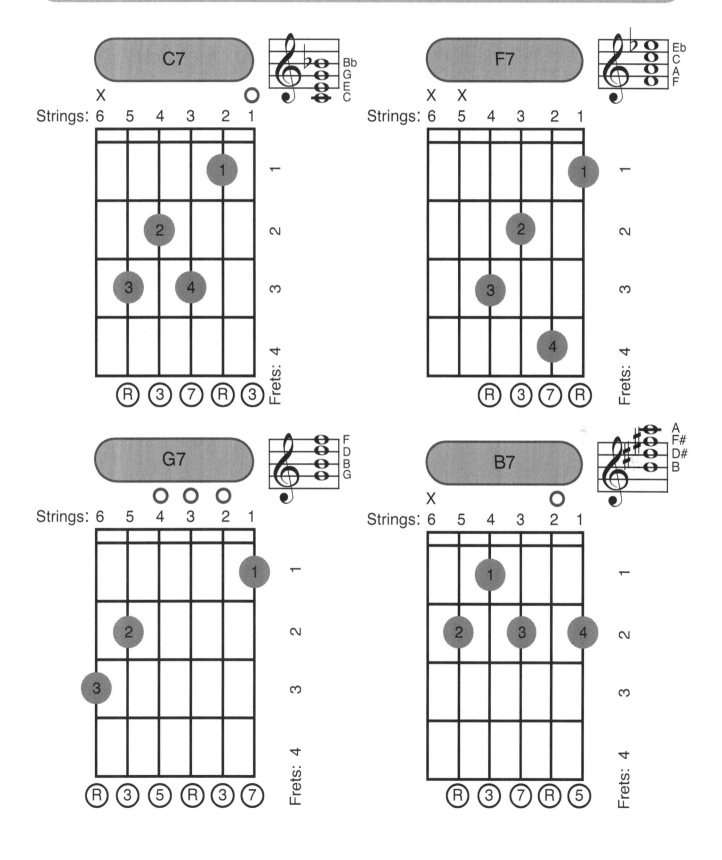

Lesson 18
12-Bar Blues Progression

In C

12-Bar Blues

Chord:	C7				C7				C7				C7			
Strum: (Beat)	1	2	3	4	1	2	3	4	1	2	3	4	1	2	3	4

Chord:	F7				F7				C7				C7			
Strum: (Beat)	1	2	3	4	1	2	3	4	1	2	3	4	1	2	3	4

Chord:	G7				F7				C7				C7			
Strum: (Beat)	1	2	3	4	1	2	3	4	1	2	3	4	1	2	3	4

Blues in C

+ Here is a 12-Bar Blues in the key of C.

+ First, try strumming for all 4 beats in each measure.

+ Next, try strumming only the 1st beat of each measure, while counting the beats aloud or in your head. For example, count "1, 2, 3, 4, 1, 2, 3, 4, 1, 2, 3, 4..." until you get to the end of the song.

+ Finally, try the exercise mentioned above, but strum on the 1st and 3rd beats, while counting aloud or in your head.

Dominant 7ths

+ Find other songs that use these Dominant 7th Chords.

+ Try playing through the songs in this section using different strumming patterns. For example, try these:

+ Down Up Down Up

Have Fun!

What We Have Learned: Section 3

- Open-Position Dominant Seventh Chords:
  A, B, C, D, E, F, G

- *12-Bar Blues in A*

- *Rockabilly Progression*

- *12-Bar Blues in C*

- The Structure of Dominant Seventh Chords

- New Rhythms and Strumming Patterns

Check Out These Artists Who Use Dominant 7th Chords

- Stevie Ray Vaughn: *Texas Flood*

- Eric Clapton: *Crossroads*

- B.B. King: *The Thrill is Gone*

- Stray Cats: *Stray Cat Strut*

Section 4

Minor 7th Chords: Open Position

Lesson 19: Minor 7th Chords
Open Position

❖Check Out
Video Lesson 5

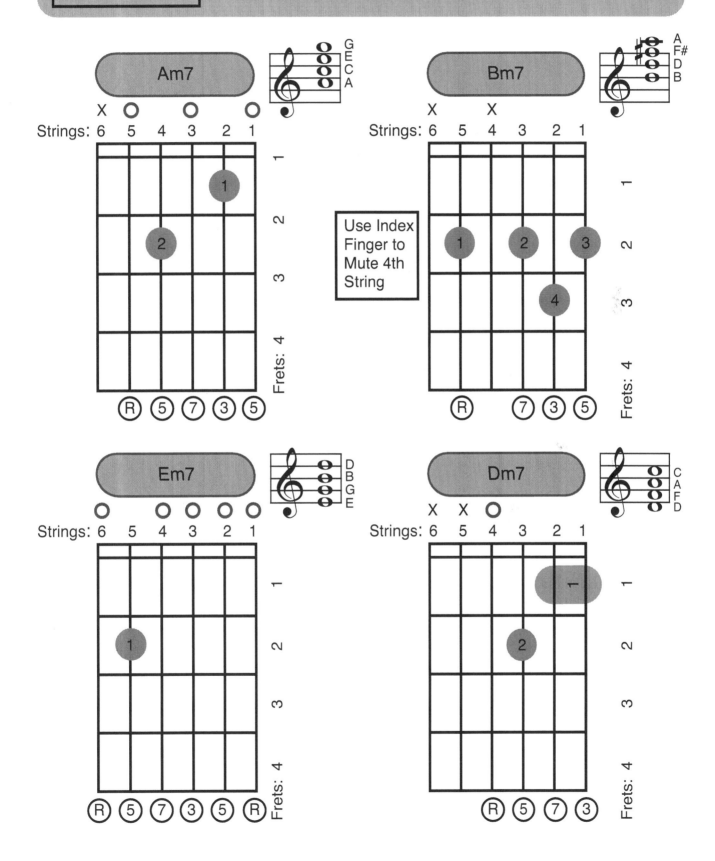

Lesson 20
Jazz / Pop Progression

Jazz in D

Chord:	D	Bm7	Em7	A7
Beat:	1 2 3 4	1 2 3 4	1 2 3 4	1 2 3 4

Chord:	D	Bm7	Em7	A7
Beat:	1 2 3 4	1 2 3 4	1 2 3 4	1 2 3 4

Chord:	G7	F7	C7	C7
Beat:	1 2 3 4	1 2 3 4	1 2 3 4	1 2 3 4

Minor 7th Chords

+ All Minor 7th Chords contain 4 notes: the Root, the 3rd, 5th and the 7th:

+ The Root is the Most Important Note. It is the Foundation for the chord, for example, C is the Root of Cm7 and G is the Root of Gm7.

+ Minor 7th Chords are often abbreviated with the Chord Letter and the Number 7. For example, Am7 and Dm7 stand for A Minor Seventh Chord and D Minor Seventh Chord.

Jazz Style

+ Minor 7th Chords are very common in Jazz.

+ For *Jazz in D*, try strumming each beat lightly with the pick.

+ For a different sound, try strumming with the side of your thumb.

+ To give a different sound color to the chords, try strumming along various locations of the neck, for example, near the bridge, over the pickups or sound hole, or near where the neck meets the body.

Lesson 21: Minor 7th Chords
Open Position

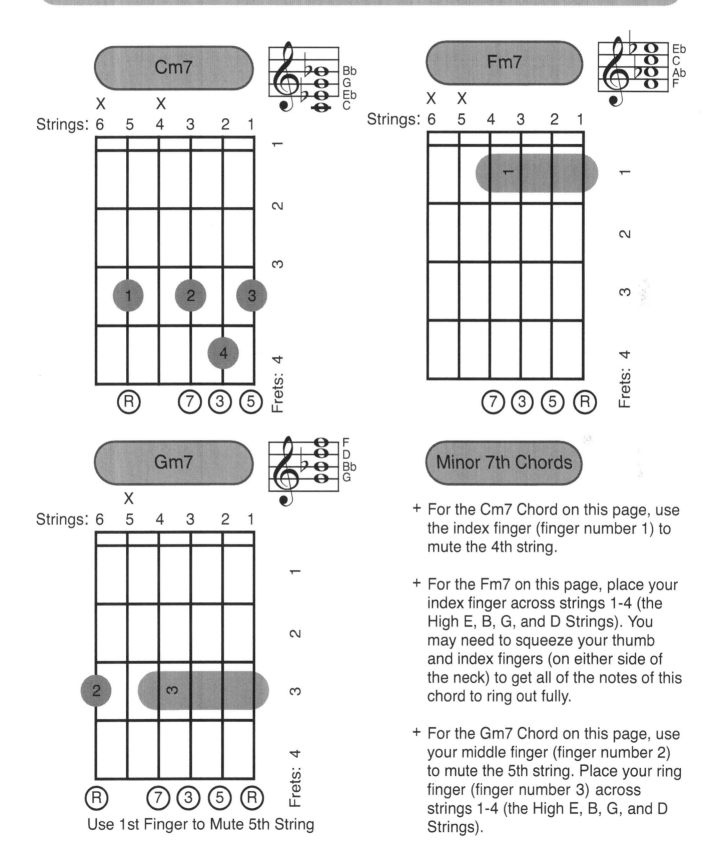

Cm7

X   X
Strings: 6 5 4 3 2 1

Bb
G
Eb
C

1   2   3
4

R   7 3 5

Frets: 4

Fm7

X X
Strings: 6 5 4 3 2 1

Eb
C
Ab
F

1

7 3 5 R

Frets: 4

Gm7

X
Strings: 6 5 4 3 2 1

F
D
Bb
G

2   3

R   7 3 5 R

Frets: 4

Use 1st Finger to Mute 5th String

Minor 7th Chords

+ For the Cm7 Chord on this page, use the index finger (finger number 1) to mute the 4th string.

+ For the Fm7 on this page, place your index finger across strings 1-4 (the High E, B, G, and D Strings). You may need to squeeze your thumb and index fingers (on either side of the neck) to get all of the notes of this chord to ring out fully.

+ For the Gm7 Chord on this page, use your middle finger (finger number 2) to mute the 5th string. Place your ring finger (finger number 3) across strings 1-4 (the High E, B, G, and D Strings).

Lesson 22: CM7 & FM7
Jazz / Pop Progression #2

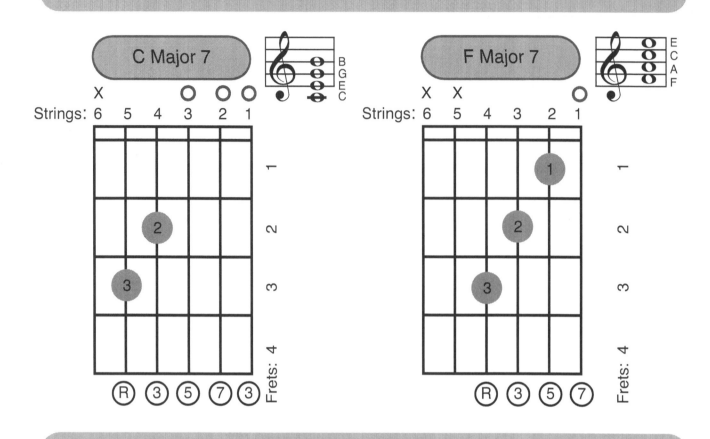

C Major 7							F Major 7					

CM7 & FM7 are Major 7th Chords

Jazz in C

Chord:	CM7				Am7				FM7				G7			
Strum:	1	2	3	4	1	2	3	4	1	2	3	4	1	2	3	4
Chord:	CM7				Am7				FM7				G7			
Strum:	1	2	3	4	1	2	3	4	1	2	3	4	1	2	3	4
Chord:	CM7				Am7				FM7				G7			
Strum:	1	2	3	4	1	2	3	4	1	2	3	4	1	2	3	4

Lesson 23
Jazz Minor Blues Progression

in A minor

Sometimes I feel like a Motherless Child

Chord:	**Am7**	**Am7**	**Dm7**	**Am7**
	Sometimes I	feel like a	motherless	child.
Strum:	1 2 3 4	1 2 3 4	1 2 3 4	1 2 3 4

Chord:	**Dm7**	**Dm7**	**E7**	**Am7**
	Sometimes I	feel like a	motherless	child.
Strum:	1 2 3 4	1 2 3 4	1 2 3 4	1 2 3 4

Chord:	**Am7**	**Am7**	**Dm7**	**Am7**
	Sometimes I	feel like a	motherless	child. A-
Strum:	1 2 3 4	1 2 3 4	1 2 3 4	1 2 3 4

Chord:	**FM7**	**Am7**	**E7**	**Am7**
	long	way from	home.	A-
Strum:	1 2 3 4	1 2 3 4	1 2 3 4	1 2 3 4

Chord:	**FM7**	**Am7**	**E7**	**Am7**
	long	way from	home.	
Strum:	1 2 3 4	1 2 3 4	1 2 3 4	1 2 3 4

1. Try strumming on all 4 beats of each measure.

2. Next, try strumming on only the first beat of each measure.

What We Have Learned: Section 4

- Open-Position Minor Seventh Chords:

  A, B, C, D, E, F, G

- *Jazz / Pop Progression*

- *Jazz in C*

- *Sometimes I Feel Like a Motherless Child*

- The Structure of Minor Seventh Chords

- New Strumming Patterns

Check Out These Artists Who Use Minor 7th Chords

- Jimi Hendrix: *Little Wing*

- Danny Gatton: *In My Room*

- Steely Dan: *Kid Charlemagne*

- Dave Matthews Band: *The Best of What's Around*

Section 5

Moveable
Major Chords

Lesson 24:
Notes on the 3rd String

The 3rd String

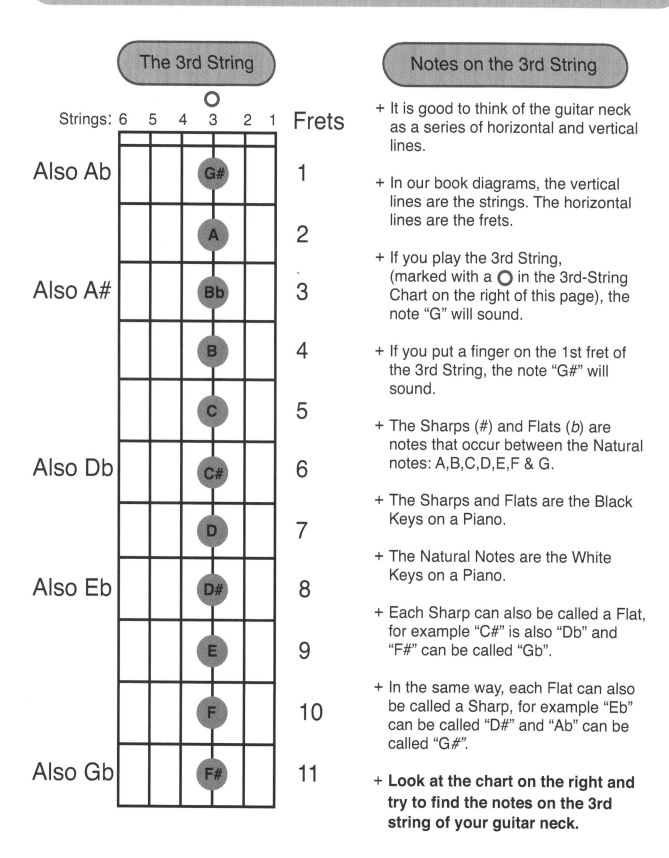

Strings: 6 5 4 3 2 1   Frets

Also Ab	G# — 1
	A — 2
Also A#	Bb — 3
	B — 4
	C — 5
Also Db	C# — 6
	D — 7
Also Eb	D# — 8
	E — 9
	F — 10
Also Gb	F# — 11

Notes on the 3rd String

+ It is good to think of the guitar neck as a series of horizontal and vertical lines.

+ In our book diagrams, the vertical lines are the strings. The horizontal lines are the frets.

+ If you play the 3rd String, (marked with a ◯ in the 3rd-String Chart on the right of this page), the note "G" will sound.

+ If you put a finger on the 1st fret of the 3rd String, the note "G#" will sound.

+ The Sharps (#) and Flats (b) are notes that occur between the Natural notes: A,B,C,D,E,F & G.

+ The Sharps and Flats are the Black Keys on a Piano.

+ The Natural Notes are the White Keys on a Piano.

+ Each Sharp can also be called a Flat, for example "C#" is also "Db" and "F#" can be called "Gb".

+ In the same way, each Flat can also be called a Sharp, for example "Eb" can be called "D#" and "Ab" can be called "G#".

+ **Look at the chart on the right and try to find the notes on the 3rd string of your guitar neck.**

Lesson 25: 3-Note Moveable Major Chords from the 3rd String

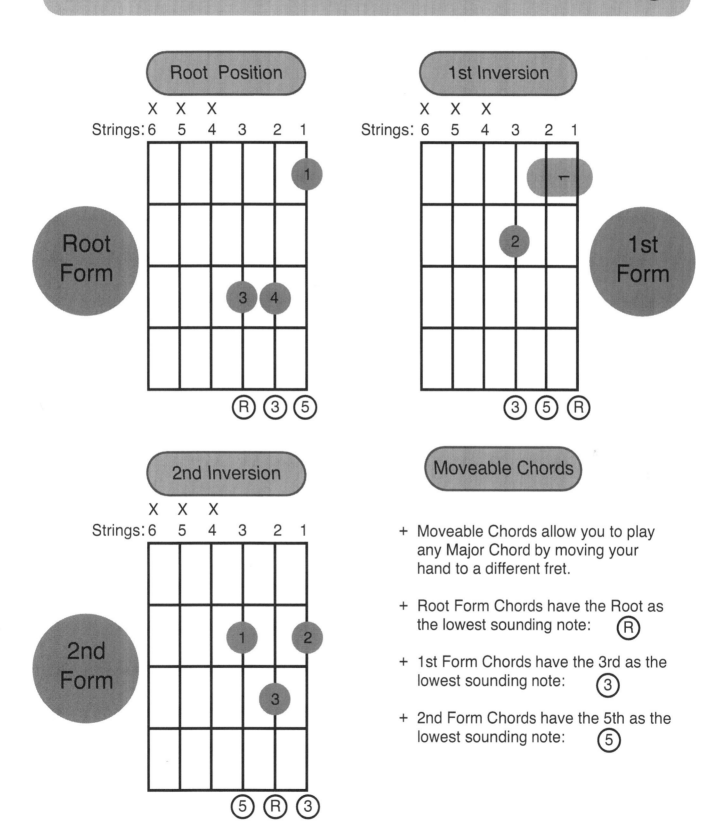

Root Position

Strings: X X X
6 5 4 3 2 1

1

3 4

R 3 5

Root Form

1st Inversion

Strings: X X X
6 5 4 3 2 1

1

2

3 5 R

1st Form

2nd Inversion

Strings: X X X
6 5 4 3 2 1

1 2

3

5 R 3

2nd Form

Moveable Chords

+ Moveable Chords allow you to play any Major Chord by moving your hand to a different fret.

+ Root Form Chords have the Root as the lowest sounding note: R

+ 1st Form Chords have the 3rd as the lowest sounding note: 3

+ 2nd Form Chords have the 5th as the lowest sounding note: 5

Lesson 26: *Amazing Grace*
Using only 2nd Form Chords

Play by using only 2nd Form Chords	*Amazing Grace*	Slide your Left Hand up and down the neck to find the position

Fret:	2nd (with Index Finger)	2nd	7th	2nd
Chord:	D	D	G	D
	A-mazing	Grace how	sweet the	sound that
Strum:	1 2 3	1 2 3	1 2 3	1 2 3

Fret:	2nd	2nd	9th	9th
Chord:	D	D	A	A
	saved a	wretch like	me.	I
Strum:	1 2 3	1 2 3	1 2 3	1 2 3

Fret:	2nd	2nd	7th	2nd
Chord:	D	D	G	D
	once was	lost but	now am	found. Was
Strum:	1 2 3	1 2 3	1 2 3	1 2 3

Fret:	2nd	9th	2nd	2nd
Chord:	D	A	D	D
	blind but	now I	see.	
Strum:	1 2 3	1 2 3	1 2 3	1 2 3

Lesson 27: *Amazing Grace*
Using All 3 Chord Forms

Amazing Grace

Use All 3 Chord Forms

in D

(with Index Finger)

Fret:	5th	5th	7th	5th
Form:	Root	Root	2nd	Root
Chord:	D	D	G	D
	A-mazing	Grace how	sweet the	sound that
Strum:	1 2 3	1 2 3	1 2 3	1 2 3

Fret:	5th	5th	5th	5th
Form:	Root	Root	1st	1st
Chord:	D	D	A	A
	saved a	wretch like	me.	I
Strum:	1 2 3	1 2 3	1 2 3	1 2 3

Fret:	5th	5th	7th	5th
Form:	Root	Root	2nd	Root
Chord:	D	D	G	D
	once was	lost but	now am	found. Was
Strum:	1 2 3	1 2 3	1 2 3	1 2 3

Fret:	5th	5th	5th	5th
Form:	Root	1st	Root	Root
Chord:	D	A	D	D
	blind but	now I	see.	
Strum:	1 2 3	1 2 3	1 2 3	1 2 3

Lesson 28:
Notes on the 4th String

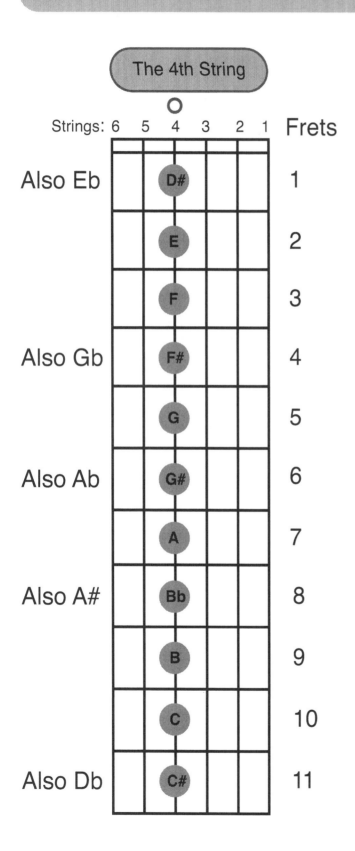

The 4th String

Strings: 6 5 4 3 2 1   Frets

Label	Note	Fret
Also Eb	D#	1
	E	2
	F	3
Also Gb	F#	4
	G	5
Also Ab	G#	6
	A	7
Also A#	Bb	8
	B	9
	C	10
Also Db	C#	11

Notes on the 4th String

+ Let's follow the format of lesson 24: Notes on the 3rd String.

+ If you play the 4th String, (marked with a O in the 4th-String Chart on the right of this page), the note "D" will sound.

+ If you put a finger on the 1st fret of the 4th String, the note "D#" will sound.

+ If you place your 1st finger on the 2nd fret of the 4th String, the note "E" will sound.

+ Try placing a finger on the 5th fret of the 4th String. This is the note "G".

+ Play the 3rd String open (letting the string vibrate). This is the note "G". Now try, once again, playing the 5th fret of the 4th String. This is also a "G". They are the same notes, although on different strings. There are many similar examples of this on the guitar: the same note on different strings.

+ Try placing a finger on the 7th fret of the 4th String. This is the note "A".

+ **Look at the chart on the right and try to find the notes on the 4th string of your guitar neck.**

Lesson 29: 3-Note Moveable Major Chords from the 4th String

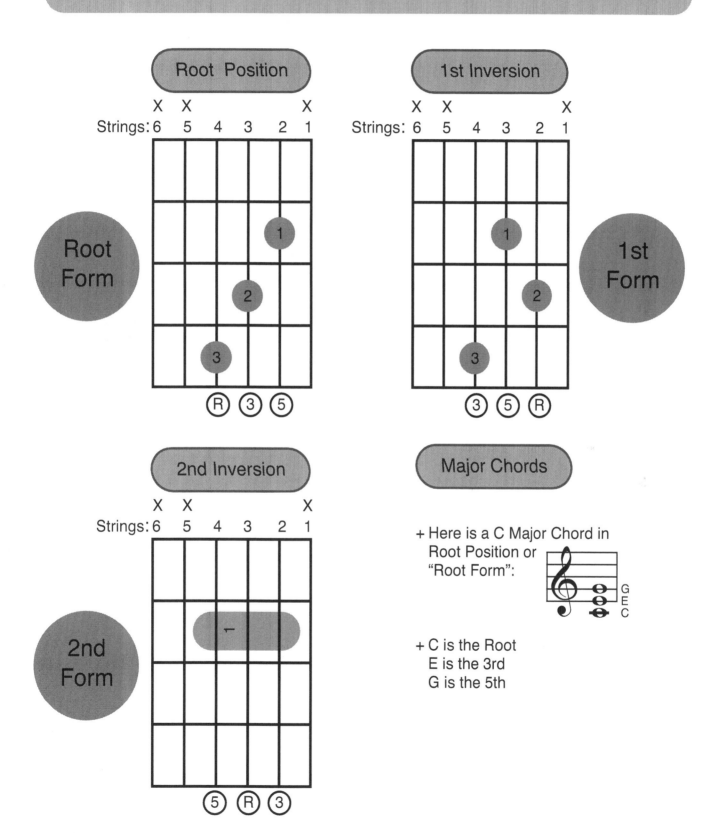

Root Position

Strings: X X X
6 5 4 3 2 1

Root Form

R 3 5

1st Inversion

Strings: X X X
6 5 4 3 2 1

1st Form

3 5 R

2nd Inversion

Strings: X X X
6 5 4 3 2 1

2nd Form

5 R 3

Major Chords

+ Here is a C Major Chord in Root Position or "Root Form":

G
E
C

+ C is the Root
  E is the 3rd
  G is the 5th

Lesson 30:
When the Saints Go Marching In

(Place Index Finger on the Fret Indicated) *When the Saints*

Fret:	**3rd**	**3rd**	**3rd**
Form:	Root	Root	Root
Chord: (No Chord)	G	G	G
Oh When the	Saints	go marchin' in	in
Strum: 1 2 3 4	1 2 3 4	1 2 3 4	1 2 3 4

Fret: 3rd	**3rd**	**3rd**	**2nd**
Form: Root	Root	Root	1st
Chord: G	G	G	D
Oh When the	Saints go	marchin'	in
Strum: 1 2 3 4	1 2 3 4	1 2 3 4	1 2 3 4

Fret: 2nd	**3rd**	**3rd**	**5th**
Form: 1st	Root	Root	2nd
Chord: D	G	G	C
Oh Lord, I	want to	be in that	number
Strum: 1 2 3 4	1 2 3 4	1 2 3 4	1 2 3 4

Fret: 5th	**3rd**	**2nd**	**3rd**
Form: 2nd	Root	1st	Root
Chord: C	G	D	G
Oh When the	Saints go	marchin'	in
Strum: 1 2 3 4	1 2 3 4	1 2 3 4	1 2 3 4

Chords for "When the Saints Go Marchin' In":

G Major Root Form: Make sure that your index finger is on the 3rd Fret of the 2nd String. This will put your left hand in the correct place on the guitar neck.

D Major 1st Form: Make sure that your index finger is on the 2nd Fret of the 3rd String. This will put your left hand in the correct place on the guitar neck.

C Major: Make sure that your index finger forms a barre across the 5th Fret of the 4th, 3rd, and 2nd Strings. This will put your left hand in the correct position.

Lesson 31:
Notes on the 5th String

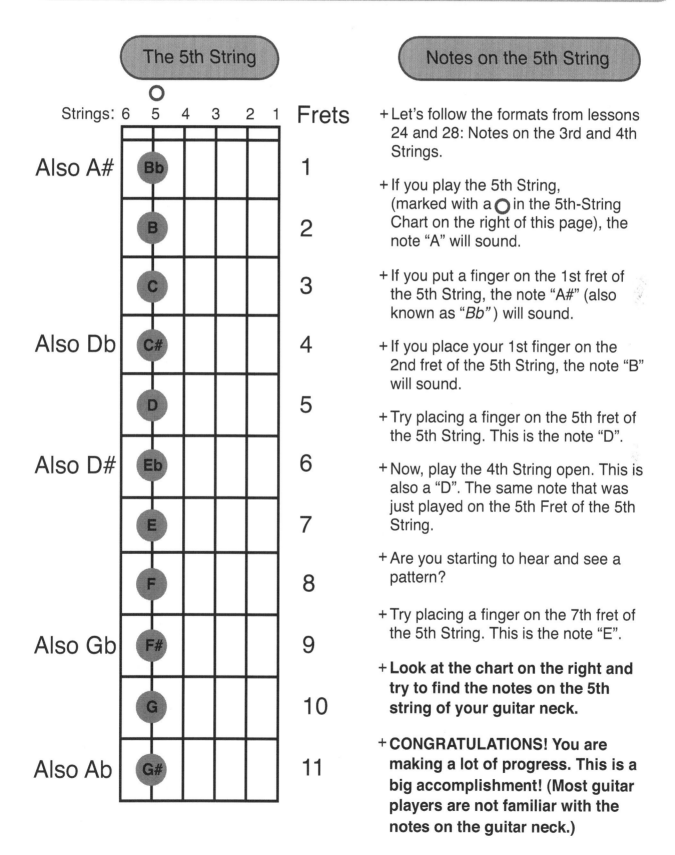

The 5th String

Strings:	6	5	4	3	2	1	Frets
Also A#		Bb					1
		B					2
		C					3
Also Db		C#					4
		D					5
Also D#		Eb					6
		E					7
		F					8
Also Gb		F#					9
		G					10
Also Ab		G#					11

Notes on the 5th String

+ Let's follow the formats from lessons 24 and 28: Notes on the 3rd and 4th Strings.

+ If you play the 5th String, (marked with a ◯ in the 5th-String Chart on the right of this page), the note "A" will sound.

+ If you put a finger on the 1st fret of the 5th String, the note "A#" (also known as "Bb") will sound.

+ If you place your 1st finger on the 2nd fret of the 5th String, the note "B" will sound.

+ Try placing a finger on the 5th fret of the 5th String. This is the note "D".

+ Now, play the 4th String open. This is also a "D". The same note that was just played on the 5th Fret of the 5th String.

+ Are you starting to hear and see a pattern?

+ Try placing a finger on the 7th fret of the 5th String. This is the note "E".

+ **Look at the chart on the right and try to find the notes on the 5th string of your guitar neck.**

+ **CONGRATULATIONS! You are making a lot of progress. This is a big accomplishment! (Most guitar players are not familiar with the notes on the guitar neck.)**

Lesson 32: 3-Note Moveable Major Chords from the 5th String

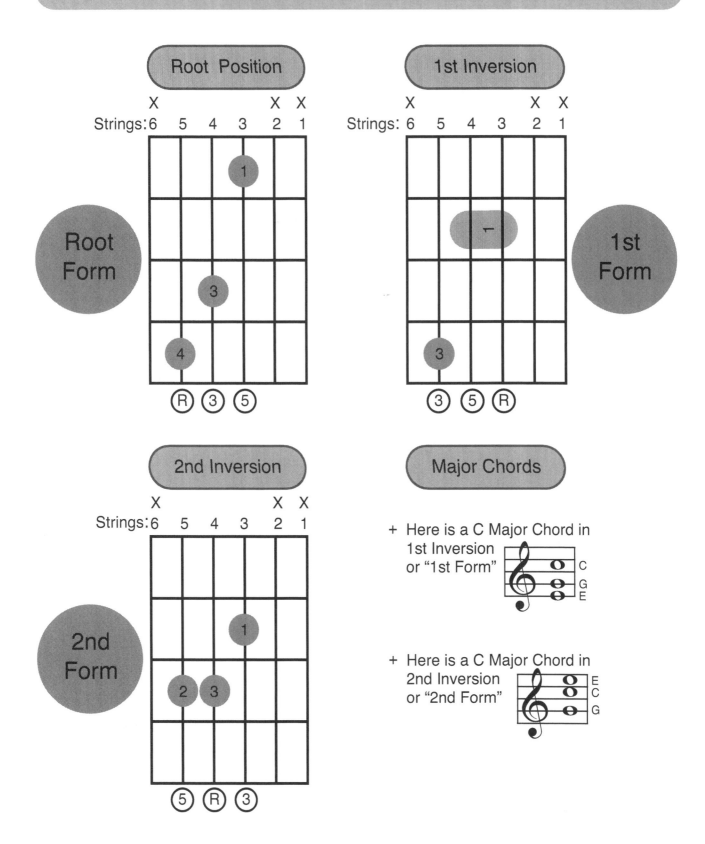

Root Position

Strings: 6 5 4 3 2 1
X   X X

Root Form

R 3 5

1st Inversion

Strings: 6 5 4 3 2 1
X   X X

1st Form

3 5 R

2nd Inversion

Strings: 6 5 4 3 2 1
X   X X

2nd Form

5 R 3

Major Chords

+ Here is a C Major Chord in 1st Inversion or "1st Form"

C
G
E

+ Here is a C Major Chord in 2nd Inversion or "2nd Form"

E
C
G

Lesson 33:
5th-String Major Chords

Peace Like a River

Chord: (No Chord)	E	E	A
I've got	peace like a	river I've got	Peace like a
Strum: 1 2 3 4	1 2 3 4	1 2 3 4	1 2 3 4
Chord: E	E	E	B
river I've got	peace like a	river in my	soul
Strum: 1 2 3 4	1 2 3 4	1 2 3 4	1 2 3 4
Chord: B	E	E	A
I've got	Peace like a	river I've got	peace like a
Strum: 1 2 3 4	1 2 3 4	1 2 3 4	1 2 3 4
Chord: E	E	B	E
river I've got	peace like a	river in my	soul
Strum: 1 2 3 4	1 2 3 4	1 2 3 4	1 2 3 4

Try out *Peace Like a River* with each of the Chord Forms (Root, 1st, and 2nd).
They are listed below.

Chord Positions for "Peace like a River"

Root Forms:
    E: Index finger on the 4th Fret of the 3rd String
    A: Index finger on the 9th Fret of the 3rd String.
    B: Index finger on the 11th Fret of the 3rd String.

1st Forms:
    E: Index finger barre on the 9th Fret of the 3rd and 4th Strings
    A: Index finger barre on the 2nd Fret of the 3rd and 4th Strings
    B: Index finger barre on the 4th Fret of the 3rd and 4th Strings

2nd Forms:
    E: Index finger on the 1st Fret of the 3rd String (Open Position Form)
    A: Index finger on the 6th Fret of the 3rd String
    B: Index finger on the 8th Fret of the 3rd String

Lesson 34:
Notes on the 6th String

The 6th String

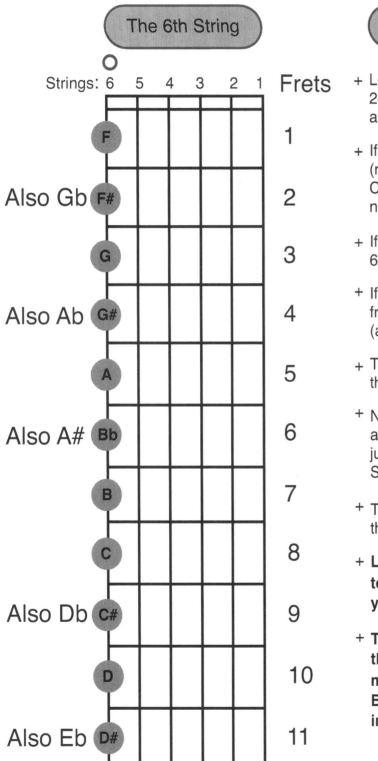

Strings: 6 5 4 3 2 1   **Frets**

Fret	Note
1	F
2	F# (Also Gb)
3	G
4	G# (Also Ab)
5	A
6	Bb (Also A#)
7	B
8	C
9	C# (Also Db)
10	D
11	D# (Also Eb)

Notes on the 6th String

+ Let's follow the formats from lessons 24, 28, and 31: Notes on the 3rd, 4th, and 5th Strings.

+ If you play the 6th String, (marked with a ○ in the 6th-String Chart on the right of this page), the note "E" will sound.

+ If you put a finger on the 1st fret of the 6th String, the note "F" will sound.

+ If you place your 1st finger on the 2nd fret of the 6th String, the note "F#" (also called "Gb") will sound.

+ Try placing a finger on the 5th fret of the 6th String. This is the note "A".

+ Now, play the 5th String open. This is also an "A". The same note that was just played on the 5th Fret of the 6th String.

+ Try placing a finger on the 7th fret of the 6th String. This is the note "B".

+ **Look at the chart on the right and try to find the notes on the 6th string of your guitar neck.**

+ **Take your time to learn the notes of the 6th String. These notes are the most useful in locating and playing Barre and Power Chords (coming up in a few pages).**

Lesson 35: 3-Note Moveable Major Chords: from the 6th String

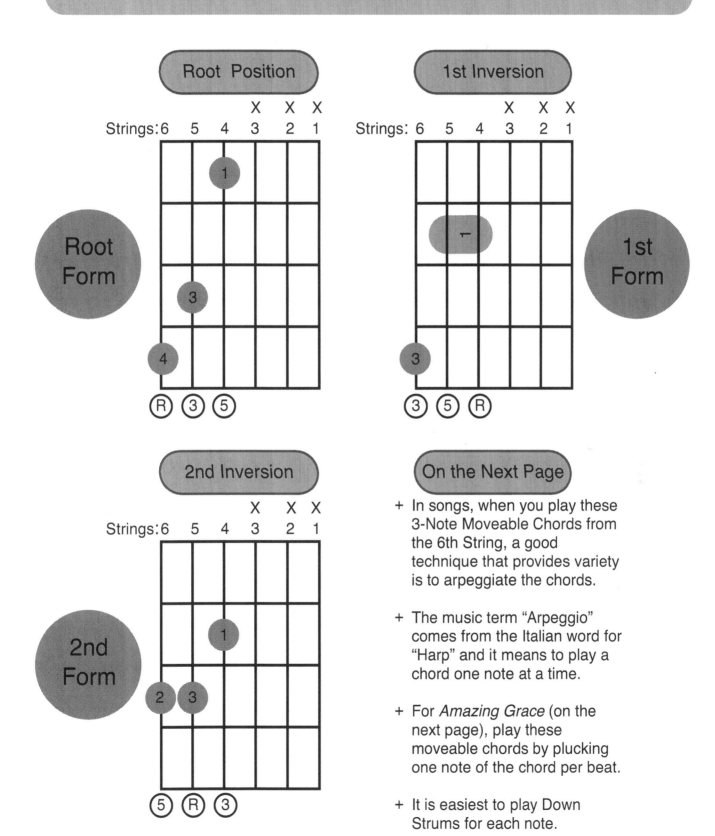

Root Position

Strings: 6 5 4 3 2 1
          X X X

Root Form

(R) (3) (5)

1st Inversion

Strings: 6 5 4 3 2 1
                X X X

1st Form

(3) (5) (R)

2nd Inversion

Strings: 6 5 4 3 2 1
                X X X

2nd Form

(5) (R) (3)

On the Next Page

+ In songs, when you play these 3-Note Moveable Chords from the 6th String, a good technique that provides variety is to arpeggiate the chords.

+ The music term "Arpeggio" comes from the Italian word for "Harp" and it means to play a chord one note at a time.

+ For *Amazing Grace* (on the next page), play these moveable chords by plucking one note of the chord per beat.

+ It is easiest to play Down Strums for each note.

Lesson 36: *Amazing Grace*
Using Plucked Chords

| All the Chords Start on the 6th String | *Amazing Grace* | | Place your Index Finger on the Fret Indicated |

Fret: 2nd	2nd	4th	2nd
Form: Root	Root	2nd	Root
Chord: A	A	D	A
A-mazing	Grace how	sweet the	sound that
Strum: 1　2　3	1　2　3	1　2　3	1　2　3
Fret: 2nd	2nd	2nd	2nd
Form: Root	Root	1st	1st
Chord: A	A	E	E
saved　a	wretch like	me.	I
Strum: 1　2　3	1　2　3	1　2　3	1　2　3
Fret: 2nd	2nd	4th	2nd
Form: Root	Root	2nd	Root
Chord: A	A	D	A
once was	lost　but	now　am	found. Was
Strum: 1　2　3	1　2　3	1　2　3	1　2　3
Fret: 2nd	2nd	2nd	2nd
Form: Root	1st	Root	Root
Chord: A	E	A	A
blind　but	now　I	see.	
Strum: 1　2　3	1　2　3	1　2　3	1　2　3

Lesson 37: Power Chords

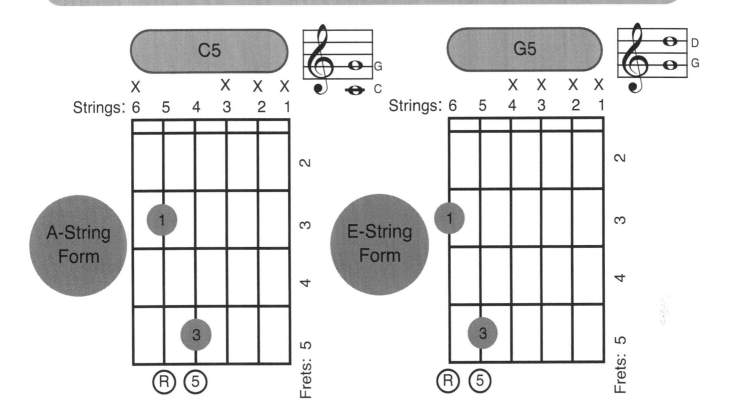

C5   G

A-String Form

G5   D   G

E-String Form

Power Chords

• Power Chords, in general, are 2-note chords
  that are used in guitar-oriented music that
  has a driving beat.

• Power Chords are made up of the Root and 5th
  of the chord. The 3rd of the chord is usually
  not played.

• The two chords depicted above are the most
  common forms of power chords. These forms
  can be moved up and down the neck just like the
  other moveable chord forms found in this book.

Lesson 37: Power Chords, Part 2 & *Rock Progression*

Palm Muting

• As you strum these chords, try gently placing your right-hand palm on top of the strings. This will dampen the sound and change its character.

• Try strumming the power chords in the first line <u>without</u> palm muting and in the second line <u>with</u> palm muting.

• Try strumming beats 1 and 2 (the first two beats of each measure) with palm muting. Then, lift your right hand up and play beats 3 and 4 (the last two beats of each measure) without palm muting.

• Experiment with different combinations of palm muting.

Index Finger on the 3rd Fret	*Rock in C*							

Chord:	C5		C5		G5		G5	
Strum:	1 2 3 4		1 2 3 4		1 2 3 4		1 2 3 4	
Chord:	C5		C5		G5		G5	
Strum:	1 2 3 4		1 2 3 4		1 2 3 4		1 2 3 4	

What We Have Learned: Section 5

- Notes on the 3rd String
- Notes on the 4th String
- Notes on the 5th String
- Notes on the 6th String
- Moveable Major Chords from the 3rd String
- Moveable Major Chords from the 4th String
- Moveable Major Chords from the 5th String
- Moveable Major Chords from the 6th String
- Power Chords

Check Out These Artists Who Use Power Chords

- Dire Straits: *Money For Nothing*
- Adele: *Rolling In the Deep*
- The Who: *We Won't Get Fooled Again*
- Van Halen: *Ain't Talkin' 'Bout Love*

Section 6

Moveable
Minor Chords

Lesson 38: 3-Note Moveable Minor Chords from the 3rd String

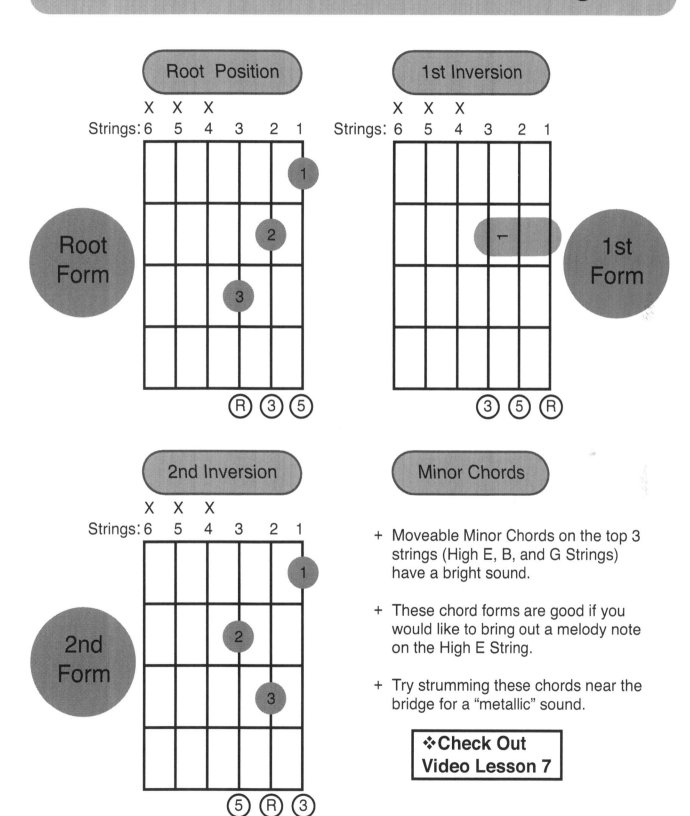

Root Position

X X X
Strings: 6 5 4 3 2 1

Root Form

Ⓡ ③ ⑤

1st Inversion

X X X
Strings: 6 5 4 3 2 1

1st Form

③ ⑤ Ⓡ

2nd Inversion

X X X
Strings: 6 5 4 3 2 1

2nd Form

⑤ Ⓡ ③

Minor Chords

+ Moveable Minor Chords on the top 3 strings (High E, B, and G Strings) have a bright sound.

+ These chord forms are good if you would like to bring out a melody note on the High E String.

+ Try strumming these chords near the bridge for a "metallic" sound.

❖Check Out
Video Lesson 7

Lesson 39: Funk- & Reggae-Style Chords

- To create a Funk-Style strumming pattern, strum an up / down pattern twice, very fast, using the **1st Form**

- To create a Reggae-Style strumming pattern, palm mute the 1st & 3rd beats and do up-strums on the 2nd and 4th beats.
- M = Mute
- ↑ = Up-strum pattern

Funk-Style Chords

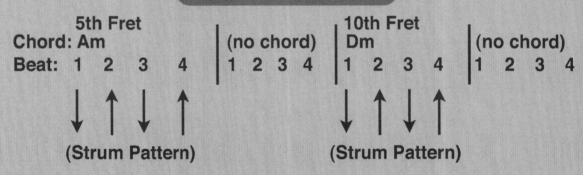

5th Fret
Chord: Am   (no chord)   10th Fret Dm   (no chord)
Beat: 1 2 3 4   1 2 3 4   1 2 3 4   1 2 3 4

↓ ↑ ↓ ↑   ↓ ↑ ↓ ↑

(Strum Pattern)   (Strum Pattern)

* 1st Form for all of the Chords.

Index Finger on the Fret Indicated

Reggae-Style Chords

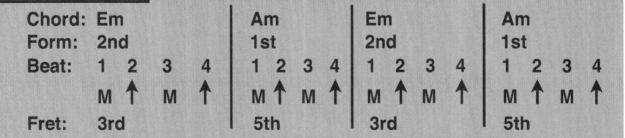

Chord:	Em	Am	Em	Am
Form:	2nd	1st	2nd	1st
Beat:	1 2 3 4	1 2 3 4	1 2 3 4	1 2 3 4
	M ↑ M ↑	M ↑ M ↑	M ↑ M ↑	M ↑ M ↑
Fret:	3rd	5th	3rd	5th

Lesson 40: 3-Note Moveable Minor Chords from the 4th String

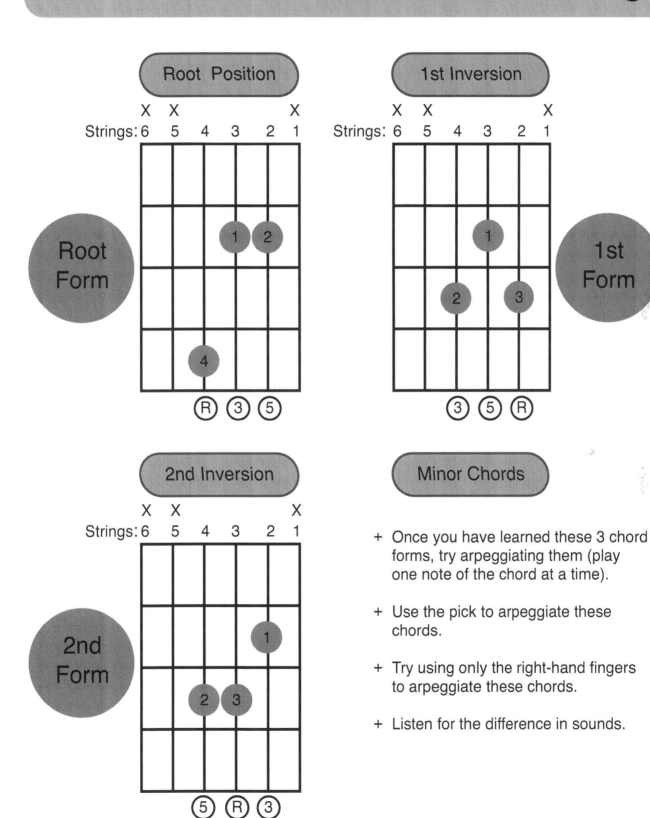

Root Position

Strings: 6 5 4 3 2 1

X X   X

Root Form

R 3 5

1st Inversion

Strings: 6 5 4 3 2 1

X X   X

1st Form

3 5 R

2nd Inversion

Strings: 6 5 4 3 2 1

X X   X

2nd Form

5 R 3

Minor Chords

+ Once you have learned these 3 chord forms, try arpeggiating them (play one note of the chord at a time).

+ Use the pick to arpeggiate these chords.

+ Try using only the right-hand fingers to arpeggiate these chords.

+ Listen for the difference in sounds.

Lesson 41: Contrasting Moveable & Open Position Chords

To create variety in songs, try alternating between moveable and open position chords.

- In *House of the Rising Sun,* try strumming 1st-Form Moveable Chords for the Minor Chords in lines 1 & 2. For the Major Chords in lines 1 & 2, use the 2nd-Form Major Chords from Lesson 29. Then, for lines 3 & 4, try strumming Open Position Chords. Listen for the difference in sounds between these two chord forms.
- Next, try sliding into the Moveable Chords from one fret below. For example, for the C Chord in measure 2, slide from the 4th to the 5th fret.

---

* From Lesson 29

House of the Rising Sun

Index Finger on the Fret Indicated

Moveable Chord:	Am	C	D	F
Fret:	9th	5th*	7th*	10th*
Beat:	1 2 3	1 2 3	1 2 3	1 2 3
Moveable Chord:	Am	C	E	E
Fret:	9th	5th*	9th*	9th*
Beat:	1 2 3	1 2 3	1 2 3	1 2 3
Open Chord:	Am	C	D	F
Beat:	1 2 3	1 2 3	1 2 3	1 2 3
Open Chord:	Am	E	Am	Am
Beat:	1 2 3	1 2 3	1 2 3	1 2 3

Lesson 42: 3-Note Moveable Minor Chords from the 5th String

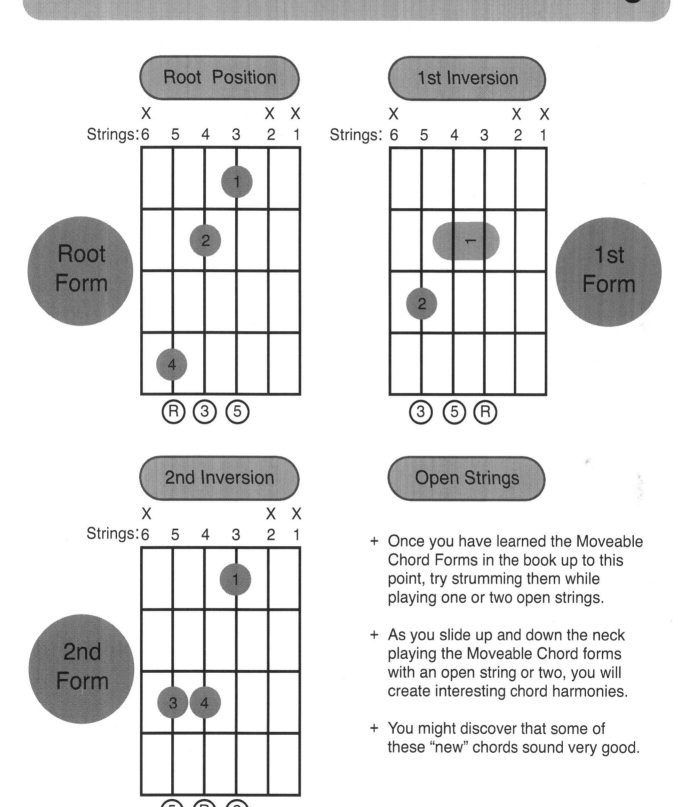

Root Position

Strings: 6 5 4 3 2 1

X   X X

Root Form

Ⓡ ③ ⑤

1st Inversion

Strings: 6 5 4 3 2 1

X   X X

1st Form

③ ⑤ Ⓡ

2nd Inversion

Strings: 6 5 4 3 2 1

X   X X

2nd Form

⑤ Ⓡ ③

Open Strings

+ Once you have learned the Moveable Chord Forms in the book up to this point, try strumming them while playing one or two open strings.

+ As you slide up and down the neck playing the Moveable Chord forms with an open string or two, you will create interesting chord harmonies.

+ You might discover that some of these "new" chords sound very good.

Lesson 43: Switching Between Moveable, 5th-String Chords

For the Major Chords, use the forms found in Lesson 32

Scarborough Fair

Place Index Finger on the Fret Indicated

Chord:	Em	G	D	Em	Em
Fret:	4th	4th	2nd	4th	4th
Form	Root	2nd	Root	Root	Root
	Are you	going to	Scarborough	Fair?	
Beat:	1 2 3	1 2 3	1 2 3	1 2 3	1 2 3

Chord:	G	Em	A	Em	Em
Fret:	4th	4th	6th	4th	4th
Form:	2nd	Root	2nd	Root	Root
	Parsley	Sage Rose-	mary and	thyme	Oh,
Beat:	1 2 3	1 2 3	1 2 3	1 2 3	1 2 3

Chord:	Em	G	C	D	D
Fret:	4th	4th	5th	7th	7th
Form:	Root	2nd	1st	1st	1st
	send my	love to	one who lives	there.	For
Beat:	1 2 3	1 2 3	1 2 3	1 2 3	1 2 3

Chord:	Em	D	C	Em	Em
Fret:	4th	2nd	5th	4th	4th
Form:	Root	Root	1st	Root	Root
	she once	was a	true love of	mine.	
Beat:	1 2 3	1 2 3	1 2 3	1 2 3	1 2 3

Lesson 44: 3-Note Moveable Minor Chords from the 6th String

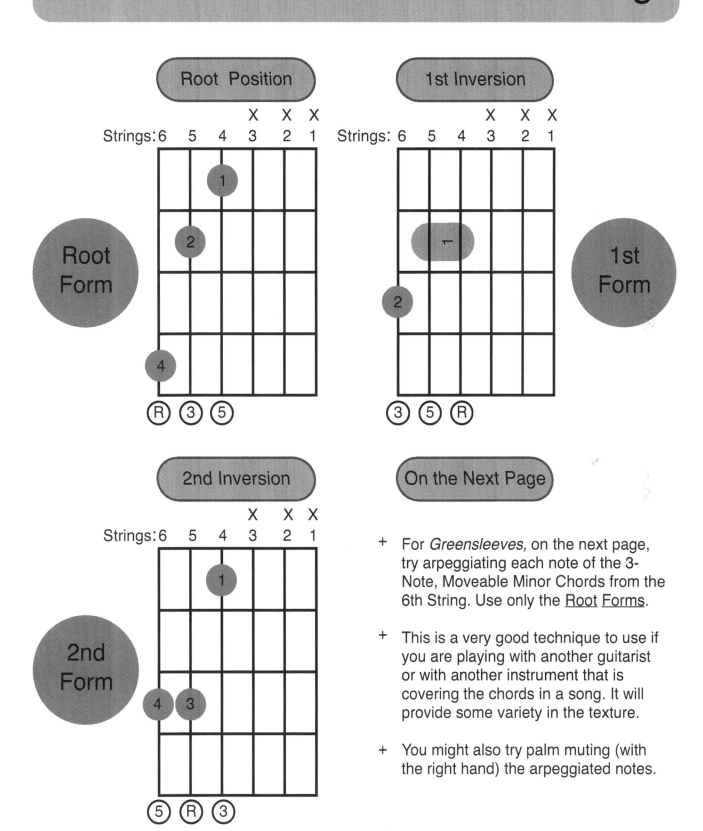

Root Position

Root Form

Strings: 6 5 4 3 2 1
X X X

1st Inversion

1st Form

Strings: 6 5 4 3 2 1
X X X

2nd Inversion

2nd Form

Strings: 6 5 4 3 2 1
X X X

On the Next Page

+ For *Greensleeves,* on the next page, try arpeggiating each note of the 3-Note, Moveable Minor Chords from the 6th String. Use only the Root Forms.

+ This is a very good technique to use if you are playing with another guitarist or with another instrument that is covering the chords in a song. It will provide some variety in the texture.

+ You might also try palm muting (with the right hand) the arpeggiated notes.

Lesson 45: *Greensleeves Using Arpeggiated Chords*

	Greensleeves		Index Finger on the Fret Indicated	
Verse Section				

Chord: Am	Am	G	G	Am
Fret: 2nd	2nd	Open	Open	2nd
Strum: 1 2 3	1 2 3	1 2 3	1 2 3	1 2 3

Chord: Am	E	E	Am	Am
Fret: 2nd	9th	9th	2nd	2nd
Strum: 1 2 3	1 2 3	1 2 3	1 2 3	1 2 3

Chord: G	G	Am	E
Open	Open	2nd	9th
Strum: 1 2 3	1 2 3	1 2 3	1 2 3

Chord: Am	Am
2nd	2nd
Strum: 1 2 3	1 2 3

Chorus Section

Chord: C	C	G	G
5th	5th	Open	Open
Strum: 1 2 3	1 2 3	1 2 3	1 2 3

Chord: Am	Am	E	E
2nd	2nd	9th	9th
Strum: 1 2 3	1 2 3	1 2 3	1 2 3

Chord: C	C	G	G
5th	5th	Open	Open
Strum: 1 2 3	1 2 3	1 2 3	1 2 3

Chord: Am	E	Am	Am
2nd	9th	2nd	2nd
Strum: 1 2 3	1 2 3	1 2 3	1 2 3

What We Have Learned: Section 6

- Funk-Style Guitar Chords

- Reggae-Style Guitar Chords

- Root-, 1st-, and Second-Position Minor Chords

- Moveable Major Chords from the 3rd String

- Moveable Major Chords from the 4th String

- Moveable Major Chords from the 5th String

- Moveable Major Chords from the 6th String

- Switching between Moveable and Open Chords

Check Out These Artists Who Use Minor Chords

- Bob Marley: *Jamming*

- Led Zeppelin: *Stairway to Heaven*

- Guns N' Roses: *Sweet Child O' Mine*

- The Rolling Stones: *Paint It Black*

Section 7

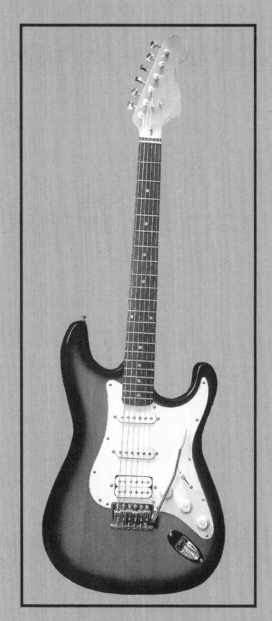

Barre
Chords

❖Check Out
Video Lesson 8

Lesson 46:
Major Barre Chords

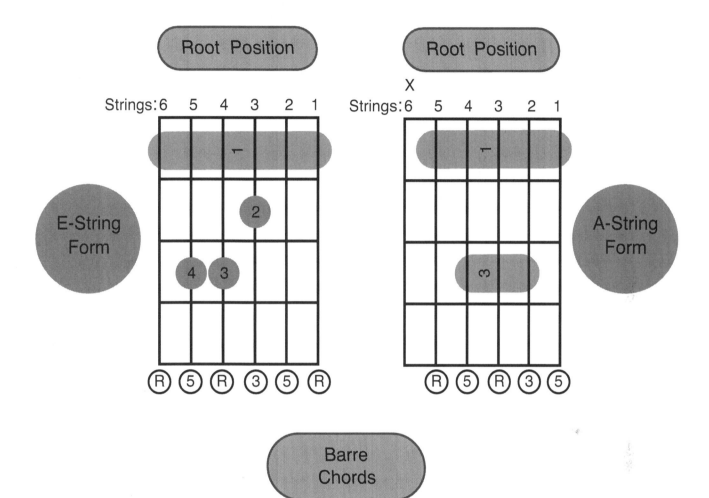

Root Position

Root Position

Strings: 6 5 4 3 2 1

X

Strings: 6 5 4 3 2 1

E-String Form

A-String Form

Barre Chords

- For Barre Chords, the Index Finger (Finger Number 1) is placed over 5 or 6 Strings.
- These Chords are very helpful, since they are full-sounding, Moveable Chords.
- They do require a fair amount of finger strength.
- So, take your time in practicing them.
- It is best to start with the index finger "clamp" and then gradually add the notes of the chord.

Lesson 47: *Peace Like a River* using Major Barre Chords

Barre-Chord Positions for *Peace Like a River*

E-String Forms:

- **A** : Index finger on the 5th Fret
- **B** : Index finger on the 7th Fret
- **E** : Open Position (no Barre Chord)

A-String Forms:

- **A** : Open Position (no Barre Chord)
- **B** : Index finger on the 2nd Fret
- **E** : Index finger on the 7th Fret

Peace Like a River

Chord:	(No Chord)		E		E		A	
	I've got		peace like a		river. I've got		Peace like a	
Strum: 1 2 3 4			1 2 3 4		1 2 3 4		1 2 3 4	

Chord: E		E		E		B	
river. I've got		peace like a		river in my		soul.	
Strum: 1 2 3 4		1 2 3 4		1 2 3 4		1 2 3 4	

Chord: B		E		E		A	
I've got		Peace like a		river. I've got		peace like a	
Strum: 1 2 3 4		1 2 3 4		1 2 3 4		1 2 3 4	

Chord: E		E		B		E	
river. I've got		peace like a		river in my		soul.	
Strum: 1 2 3 4		1 2 3 4		1 2 3 4		1 2 3 4	

Lesson 48: Minor Barre Chords

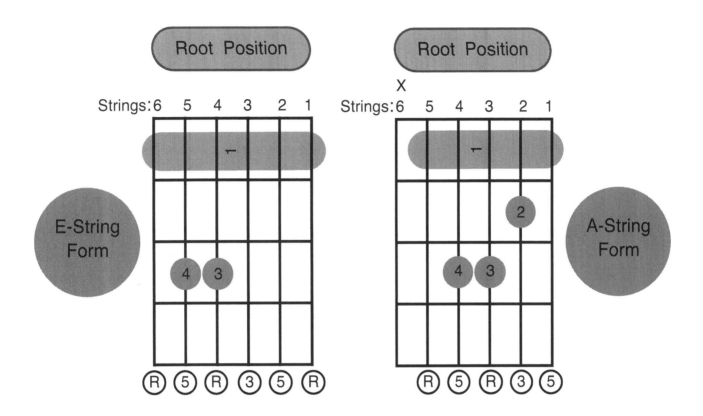

- For Minor Barre Chords, the Index Finger (Finger Number 1) is placed over 5 or 6 Strings.
- These Chords are very similar to the Major Barre Chord forms.
- The most common forms (shown above) are on the 6th and 5th Strings.
- Like the Major Barre Chord forms, they also require a bit of finger strength. So, take your time in practicing them.
- It is best to start with the index finger "clamp" and then gradually add the notes of the chord.

Lesson 49: *House of the Rising Sun* Using Barre Chords

Barre-Chord Positions for *House of the Rising Sun*

E-String Forms:

> **Am:** Index finger on the 5th Fret
> **C** : Index finger on the 8th Fret
> **D** : Index finger on the 10th Fret
> **F** : Index finger on the 1st Fret
> **E** : Open Position (no Barre Chord)

A-String Forms:

> **Am:** Open Position (no Barre Chord)
> **C** : Index finger on the 3rd Fret
> **D** : Index finger on the 5th Fret
> **F** : Index finger on the 8th Fret
> **E** : Index finger on the 7th Fret

House of the Rising Sun

Chord:	Am	C	D	F
	There is a	house in	New Or-	leans they
Strum:	1 2 3	1 2 3	1 2 3	1 2 3

Chord:	Am	C	E	E
	call the	ris- ing	sun.	It's
Strum:	1 2 3	1 2 3	1 2 3	1 2 3

Chord:	Am	C	D	F
	been the	ruin of	many poor	souls and
Strum:	1 2 3	1 2 3	1 2 3	1 2 3

Chord:	Am	E	Am	Am
	Lord, I	know I'm	one.	
Strum:	1 2 3	1 2 3	1 2 3	1 2 3

Lesson 50: *House of the Rising Sun*
Using Power Chords

Power-Chord Positions for *House of the Rising*

E-String Forms: Strum only the 5th and 6th Strings

    Am: Index finger on the 5th Fret
    C : Index finger on the 8th Fret
    D : Index finger on the 10th Fret
    F : Index finger on the 1st Fret
    E : Open Position (Index finger on the 2nd fret of the 5th String)

A-String Forms: Strum only the 4th and 5th Strings

    Am: Open Position (Index finger on the 2nd fret of the 4th String)
    C : Index finger on the 3rd Fret
    D : Index finger on the 5th Fret
    F : Index finger on the 8th Fret
    E : Index finger on the 7th Fret

House of the Rising Sun

Chord:	Am			C			D			F		
	There	is	a	house	in		New Or-			leans	they	
Strum:	1	2	3	1	2	3	1	2	3	1	2	3

Chord:	Am			C			E			E		
		call	the	ris-	ing		sun.				It's	
Strum:	1	2	3	1	2	3	1	2	3	1	2	3

Chord:	Am			C			D			F		
		been	the	ruin	of		many	poor		souls	and	
Strum:	1	2	3	1	2	3	1	2	3	1	2	3

Chord:	Am			E			Am			Am		
	Lord,	I		know	I'm		one.					
Strum:	1	2	3	1	2	3	1	2	3	1	2	3

Lesson 51:
Dominant 7th Barre Chords

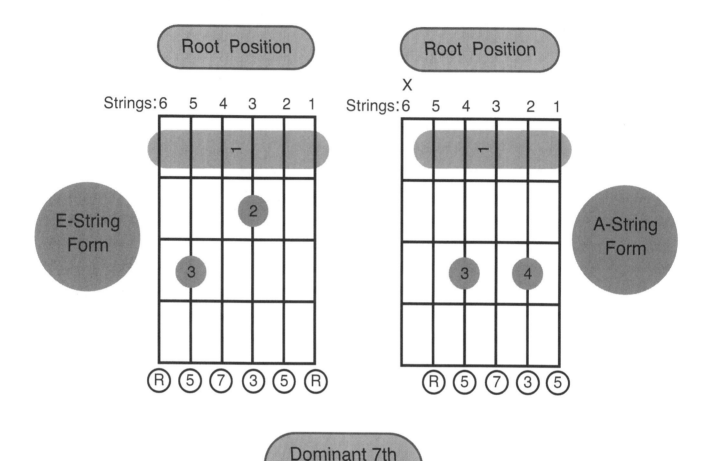

Dominant 7th Barre Chords

- For Dominant 7th Barre Chords, the Index Finger is placed over 5 or 6 Strings.
- These Chords are very helpful, since they are full-sounding, Moveable Chords.
- The E-String Form has a similar shape to the open E7 chord from Lesson 13.
- The A-String Form has a similar shape to the open A7 chord, also from Lesson 13.

Lesson 52: *Amazing Grace*
Using Dominant 7 Barre Chords

Index Finger on
the Fret Indicated

Amazing Grace

Fret:	5th	5th	3rd	5th
Form:	A-String	A-String	E-String	A-String
Chord:	D7	D7	G7	D7
	A-mazing	Grace how	sweet the	sound that
Strum:	1 2 3	1 2 3	1 2 3	1 2 3

Fret:	5th	5th	5th	5th
Form:	A-String	A-String	E-String	E-String
Chord:	D7	D7	A7	A7
	saved a	wretch like	me.	I
Strum:	1 2 3	1 2 3	1 2 3	1 2 3

Fret:	5th	5th	3rd	5th
Form:	A-String	A-String	E-String	A-String
Chord:	D7	D7	G7	D7
	once was	lost but	now am	found. Was
Strum:	1 2 3	1 2 3	1 2 3	1 2 3

Fret:	5th	5th	5th	5th
Form:	A-String	E-String	A-String	A-String
Chord:	D7	A7	D7	D7
	blind but	now I	see.	
Strum:	1 2 3	1 2 3	1 2 3	1 2 3

Lesson 53: *12-Bar Blues with Dominant 7th Barre Chords*

12-Bar Blues

Chord:	A7 (5th fret)	A7	A7	A7
Form:	E-String			
Strum:	1 2 3 4	1 2 3 4	1 2 3 4	1 2 3 4

Chord:	D7 (5th fret)	D7	A7 (5th fret)	A7
Form:	A-String		E-String	
Strum:	1 2 3 4	1 2 3 4	1 2 3 4	1 2 3 4

Chord:	E7 (7th fret)	D7 (5th fret)	A7 (5th fret)	A7
Form:	A-String	A-String	E-String	
Strum:	1 2 3 4	1 2 3 4	1 2 3 4	1 2 3 4

Fretboard Positions for *12-Bar Blues*

A7: E-String Form on the 5th Fret

D7: A-String Form on the 5th Fret

E7: A-String Form on the 7th Fret

Lesson 54:
Minor 7th Barre Chords

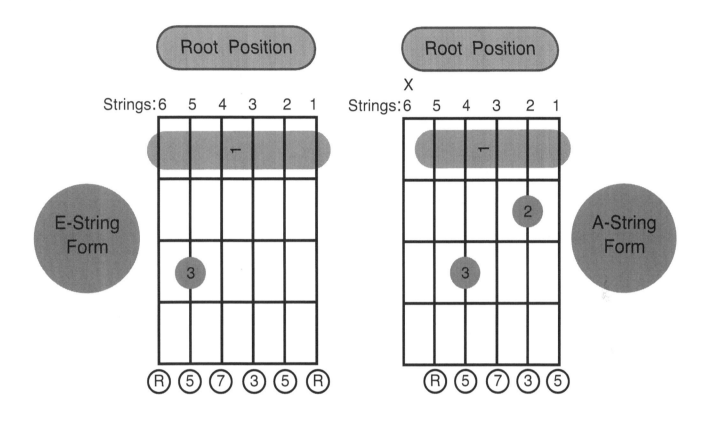

Root Position

Root Position

E-String Form

A-String Form

Strings: 6 5 4 3 2 1

Strings: 6 5 4 3 2 1

(R) (5) (7) (3) (5) (R)

(R) (5) (7) (3) (5)

Minor 7th Barre Chords

- For Minor 7th Barre Chords, the Index Finger is placed over 5 or 6 Strings.
- These Chords are very helpful, since they are full-sounding, Moveable Chords.
- The E-String Form has a similar shape to the open Em7 chord from Lesson 19.
- The A-String Form has a similar shape to the open Am7 chord, also from Lesson 19.

Lesson 55: *Jazz Minor Blues* Using Minor 7th Barre Chords

in A minor *Sometimes I feel like a Motherless Child*

Chord:	Am7	Am7	Dm7	Am7
	Sometimes I	feel like a	motherless	child.
Strum:	1 2 3 4	1 2 3 4	1 2 3 4	1 2 3 4

Chord:	Dm7	Dm7	E7	Am7
	Sometimes I	feel like a	motherless	child.
Strum:	1 2 3 4	1 2 3 4	1 2 3 4	1 2 3 4

Chord:	Am7	Am7	Dm7	Am7
	Sometimes I	feel like a	motherless	child. A-
Strum:	1 2 3 4	1 2 3 4	1 2 3 4	1 2 3 4

Chord:	F	Am7	E7	Am7
	long	way from	home.	A-
Strum:	1 2 3 4	1 2 3 4	1 2 3 4	1 2 3 4

Chord:	F	Am7	E7	Am7
	long	way from	home.	
Strum:	1 2 3 4	1 2 3 4	1 2 3 4	1 2 3 4

Fretboard Positions for the E-String Barre-Chord Forms

Am7: 5th Fret
Dm7: 10th Fret
E7:   Open Position
F: 1st Fret

Lesson 56: *When the Saints* with 7th Barre Chords

When the Saints

Fret:	**3rd**	**3rd**	**3rd**
Form:	**E-String**		
Chord: (No Chord)	**G7**	**G7**	**G7**
Oh When the	Saints	go marchin'	in
Strum: 1 2 3 4	1 2 3 4	1 2 3 4	1 2 3 4

Fret: **3rd**	**3rd**	**3rd**	**5th**
Form: **E-String**			**A-String**
Chord: **G7**	**G7**	**G7**	**D7**
Oh When the	Saints go	marchin'	in
Strum: 1 2 3 4	1 2 3 4	1 2 3 4	1 2 3 4

Fret: **5th**	**3rd**	**3rd**	**3rd**
Form: **A-String**	**E-String**	**E-String**	**A-String**
Chord: **D7**	**G7**	**G7**	**C7**
Oh Lord, I	want to	be in that	number
Strum: 1 2 3 4	1 2 3 4	1 2 3 4	1 2 3 4

Fret: **3rd**	**3rd**	**5th**	**3rd**
Form: **A-String**	**E-String**	**A-String**	**E-String**
Chord: **C7**	**G7**	**D7**	**G7**
Oh When the	Saints go	marchin'	in
Strum: 1 2 3 4	1 2 3 4	1 2 3 4	1 2 3 4

Try strumming the chords with the back side of the pick or with your thumb for a different sound.

What We Have Learned: Section 7

- 2 Basic Formats for Barre Chords:

  E-String Forms and A-String Forms

- Major Barre Chords

- Minor Barre Chords

- Dominant Seventh Barre Chords

- Minor Seventh Barre Chords

- Switching Between Barre Chords Types

Check Out These Artists Who Use Barre Chords

- The Allman Brothers: *Freebird*

- Boston: *More Than a Feeling*

- The Doors: *Light My Fire*

- Tom Petty: *American Girl*

Section 8

Major 7th Chords
Open Position

Lesson 57
Major 7th Chords: Open Position

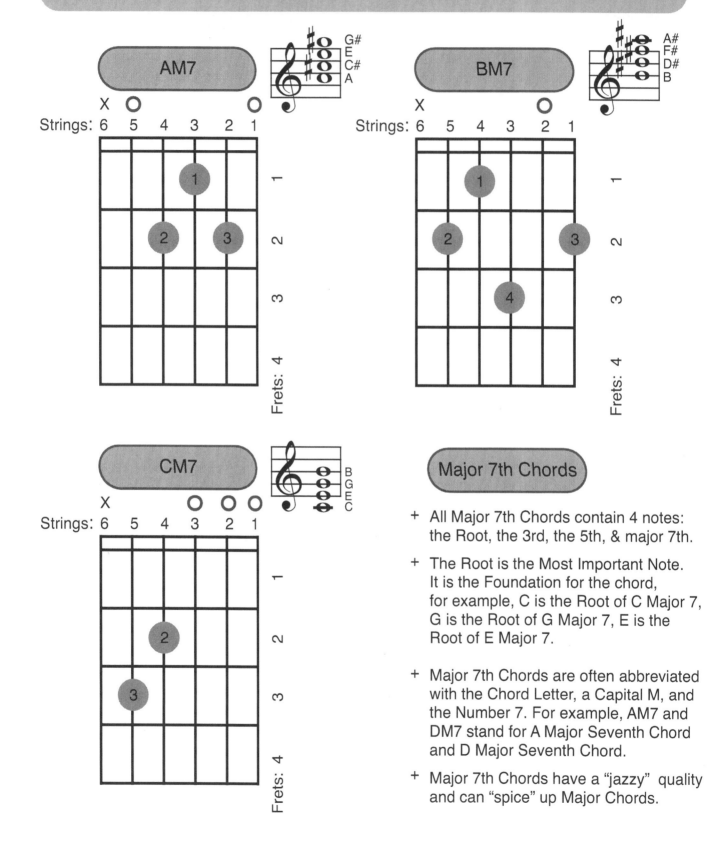

Major 7th Chords

+ All Major 7th Chords contain 4 notes: the Root, the 3rd, the 5th, & major 7th.

+ The Root is the Most Important Note. It is the Foundation for the chord, for example, C is the Root of C Major 7, G is the Root of G Major 7, E is the Root of E Major 7.

+ Major 7th Chords are often abbreviated with the Chord Letter, a Capital M, and the Number 7. For example, AM7 and DM7 stand for A Major Seventh Chord and D Major Seventh Chord.

+ Major 7th Chords have a "jazzy" quality and can "spice" up Major Chords.

Lesson 58
Major 7th Chords: Open Position

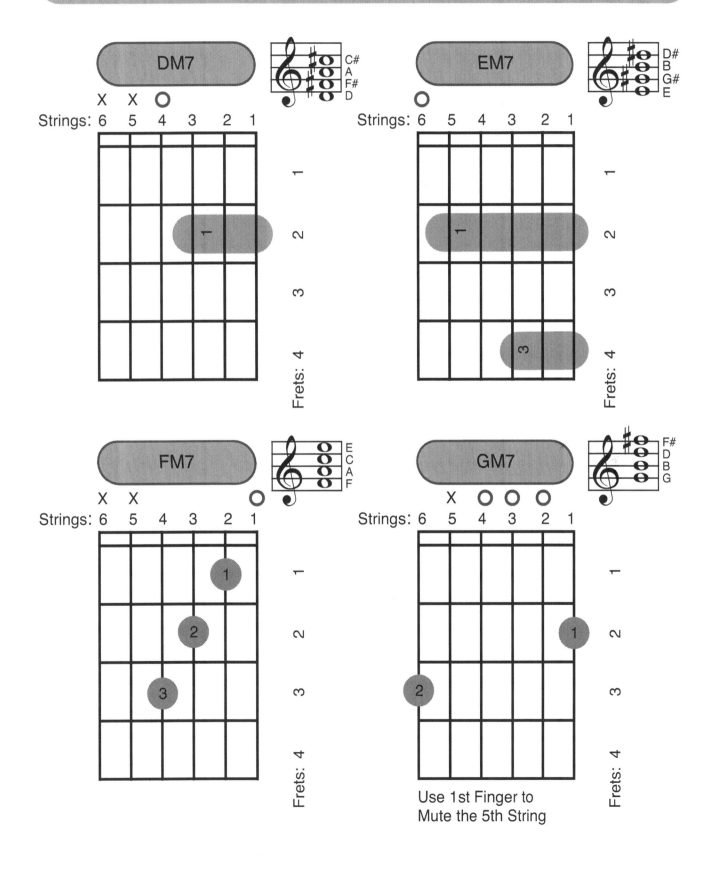

Lesson 59
Major 7th Chords: Open Position

Jazz Chords

Chord: CM7	CM7	FM7	FM7
Strum: 1 2 3 4	1 2 3 4	1 2 3 4	1 2 3 4

Chord: DM7	DM7	AM7	AM7
Strum: 1 2 3 4	1 2 3 4	1 2 3 4	1 2 3 4

Chord: EM7	EM7	BM7	BM7
Strum: 1 2 3 4	1 2 3 4	1 2 3 4	1 2 3 4

Chord: GM7	GM7	CM7	CM7
Strum: 1 2 3 4	1 2 3 4	1 2 3 4	1 2 3 4

Try playing this song at different tempi (speeds):

1. A slow tempo

2. A Moderate tempo

3. A Fast tempo

What We Have Learned: Section 8

- Major Seventh Chords in Open Position:
  A, B, C, D, E, F, G
- The Structure of Major Seventh Chords
- Major Seventh Chord Abbreviations
- Major Seventh Chords in Songs
- Playing Songs in Different Tempi (Speeds)

Check Out These Artists Who Use Major 7th Chords

- Eric Johnson: *Nothing Can Keep Me From You*
- Taylor Swift: *Never Grow Up*
- Steve Morse: *Ghost Wind*

Section 9

Augmented & Diminished Chords

Lesson 60:
Moveable Augmented Chords

Overview

+ Augmented Chords are more "advanced" than Major and Minor Chords.

+ They are based on two sets of major-third intervals.

+ Augmented Chords are often used as transitional chords between two more significant chords in a song.

+ They embellish the harmony and make more colorful progressions.

+ We will go into Augmented Chords in more detail in *Guitar Adventures 2: A Fun, Informative, and Step-By-Step 60-Lesson Guide to Scales, Chords, and Arpeggios, with Companion Lesson and Play-Along Videos*

Augmented Chords

+ All Augmented Chords contain 3 notes: the Root, the 3rd, and the 5th.

+ In Augmented Chords the distance between the Root and the 3rd is made up of 2 Major 2nds

+ In Augmented Chords the distance between the 3rd and the 5th is also made up of 2 Major 2nds

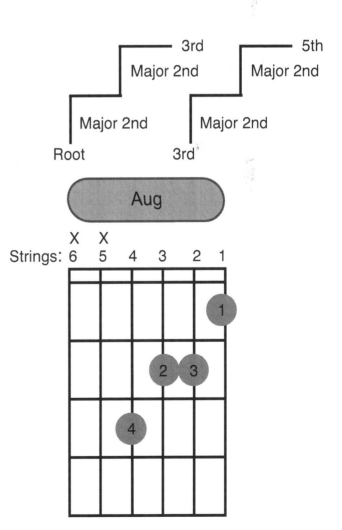

Aug

X					X
Strings: 6 5 4 3 2 1

Aug

X	X				
Strings: 6 5 4 3 2 1

Lesson 61: Moveable Diminished Chords

Overview

+ Diminished Chords are more "advanced" than Major and Minor Chords.

+ They are based on two sets of minor-third intervals.

+ Diminished Chords are often used as transitional chords between two more significant chords in a song.

+ They embellish the harmony and make more colorful progressions.

+ We will go into Diminished Chords in more detail in *Guitar Adventures 2: A Fun, Informative, and Step-By-Step 60-Lesson Guide to Scales, Chords, and Arpeggios, with Companion Lesson and Play-Along Videos*

Diminished Chords

+ All Diminished Chords contain 3 notes: the Root, the 3rd, and the 5th.

+ In Diminished Chords the distance between the Root and the 3rd is made up of 1 Major 2nd and 1 Minor 2nd.

+ In Diminished Chords the distance between the 3rd and the 5th is also made up of 1 Major 2nd and 1 Minor 2nd.

Diminished Chord Intervals

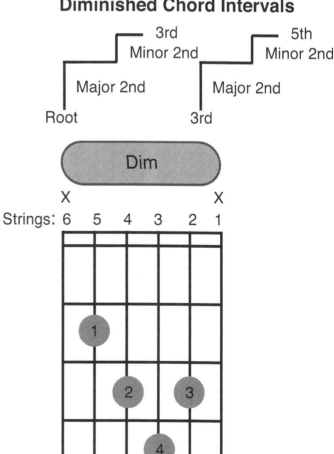

What We Have Learned: Section 9

- 2 Moveable Forms for Augmented Chords
- 2 Moveable Forms for Diminished Chords
- The Structure of Augmented Chords
- The Structure of Diminished Chords
- The Sound Character of Augmented Chords
- The Sound Character of Diminished Chords

Check Out These Artists Who Use Augmented and Diminished Chords Chords

- Queen: *Bohemian Rhapsody*
- Joe Satriani: *Ice 9*
- Shawn Lane: *Rules of the Game*

Appendix

Guitar Adventures Free Videos: Tables of Contents

Video Lesson	Lesson Page	Subject
1		Introduction: How the Book Works
2	1	Major Chords, Intervals, Measures
3	8	Minor Chords, Strumming Technique
4	13	Rockabilly Chords
5	19	Strumming in Different Neck Locations
6	24	Notes, Moveable Chords, Power Chords
7	38	Funk, Reggae, Arpeggiating Chords
8	46	Barre Chords
9	57	7th Chords
10	60	Augmented and Diminished Chords

Play-Along Video	Lesson Page	Song
1	2	*Amazing Grace*
2	4	*When the Saints Go Marchin' In*
3	5	*Peace Like a River*
4	8	*House of the Rising Sun*
5	9	*Scarborough Fair*
6	12	*Greensleeves*
7	16	*Rockabilly Progression*
8	23	*Sometimes I Feel Like a Motherless Child*

Lesson Checklist:
Page 1

Use this Checklist to Keep Track of Your Progress:

Lesson #	Completed / Check	Date
1		
2		
3		
4		
5		
6		
7		
8		
9		
10		
11		
12		
13		
14		
15		
16		
17		
18		
19		
20		

Lesson Checklist: Page 2

Use this Checklist to Keep Track of Your Progress:

Lesson #	Completed / Check	Date
21		
22		
23		
24		
25		
26		
27		
28		
29		
30		
31		
32		
33		
34		
35		
36		
37		
38		
39		
40		

Lesson Checklist: Page 3

Use this Checklist to Keep Track of Your Progress:

Lesson #	Completed / Check	Date
41		
42		
43		
44		
45		
46		
47		
48		
49		
50		
51		
52		
53		
54		
55		
56		
57		
58		
59		
60		
61		

Suggestions for Listening:

A Short (and incomplete) List of Guitarists who have an imaginative approach to chords

Jimi Hendrix

The Edge

Eric Johnson

Alan Holdsworth

Pete Townshend

Mark Knopfler

Wes Montgomery

Eddie Van Halen

Joe Pass

Michael Hedges

Tommy Emmanuel

Angus Young

James Hetfield

Robbie Robertson

Steve Morse

About the Author

Damon Ferrante is a composer, guitarist, and music writer. When he was 8 years old, his uncle left an old electric guitar, which was in two pieces (neck and body separated) at his parents' house. Damon put the guitar together using some old screws and duct tape. That was the beginning of a wild ride through Rock, Jazz, Classical Music, and Opera that has spanned over 20 years. Along the way, Ferrante has had performances at Carnegie Hall, Symphony Space, and throughout the US and Europe. He has taught on the music faculties of Seton Hall University and Montclair State University. He is the director of Steeplechase Arts & Productions, a company that he founded in 2003. Damon lives in New York City.

Acknowledgements

I am grateful to the many people who helped in the design and editing process for this book: Noah Engel and Jackson Highland-Lipski for their excellent video and photography work, Barbara Columbo for her design advice, Jason Ferrante for his insights into lesson planning, Amy and David Martin for their tech assistance, Barbara and Joe for everything else.

Dedication

This book is dedicated to the hundreds of students, over the last two decades, who have helped teach me how to play the guitar. Here is a short list: Baird and Gabe Acheson, Theo Epstein, Caleb and Josh Brooks, Teddy and Charlie Obrecht, Gabriel and Bridget Donner, Tom, Lauren, and Kim Riley, Hannah and Emma Pope, Alex and Mika Poblete, Will and Ben Gantt, Ty and Will Washburn, Brae Gromek, David and Andrew Brennan, Ylva Hellstrand, Stephan Dalal, Cyrus Alamzad, Amanda, Olivia and Kyle Shattuck, Annabelle Hu, Skyler Snow, Jasper and Teddy Martin, Jack and Sophia Algerio, Kyle Seaman, and Sully.

21564258R00051

Made in the USA
Lexington, KY
18 March 2013